The
Psychology
of Creativity
and Discovery

The Psychology of Creativity and Discovery

Scientists and Their Work

Richard S. Mansfield
and
Thomas V. Busse

Nelson-Hall [nh] Chicago

Library of Congress Cataloging in Publication Data

Mansfield, Richard S
 The psychology of creativity and discovery.

 Bibliography: p.
 Includes index.
 1. Creative ability in science. I. Busse, Thomas V., joint author. II.
Title.
Q172.5.C74M36   153.3'5'0885   80-29219
ISBN 0-88229-653-1

Manufactured in the United States of America

10   9   8   7   6   5   4   3   2   1

243679

Dedicated to our parents,
James and Sarah Mansfield
and
Louis and Ruth Busse,
and to our wives,
Mary Mansfield and Pauline Busse

Contents

Preface

THE WORD *CREATIVITY* has been applied to accomplishments as disparate as a five-year-old's drawing and
Isaac Newton's second law of motion. Psychologists
studying creativity have contributed to this semantic
diffusion: some have defined creativity in terms of real-
life accomplishments, but the majority have relied on a
profusion of tests, each ostensibly measuring a trait or
set of traits hypothesized to be central to creativity. This
diversity of definition has produced a jumble of findings
with only dubious applicability to real-life creative
performance.

We began the work that led to this book with the
conviction that the field of creativity was in a morass.
Early in 1973, in an effort to identify the critical issues
in creativity, we began an informal seminar with three
graduate students at Temple University: Cheryl Hartman, Ernest Krepelka, and Felice Platt. After six months

of discussion we focused on three topics: the criterion validity of various creativity tests; the child-rearing antecedents of creativity; and the training of creativity. We decided to review the research on these topics critically and comprehensively. Our purpose was to establish a base of knowledge upon which researchers, including ourselves, might build.

Over the next two years each review developed into a manuscript of over 100 pages. The review of the validation studies convinced us that meaningful progress in creativity research would come primarily from studies emphasizing real-life creativity. This realization soon had implications for the other two reviews. In the review of the child-rearing antecedents of creativity, we decided to focus only on studies in which creativity was measured by real-life accomplishments or related criteria. It also became clear that the creativity training studies did not fit into our emerging strategy, because they evaluated the effects of training on test performance, not on real-life attainments. Therefore, we decided to publish the review of the training studies separately.

As the review developed, our own theorizing about creativity began to evolve. Because the reviews and the theorizing shared a common focus on real-life accomplishments, especially in science, it seemed that the obvious way to present our findings was in book form. Once this decision was made, we realized that hundred-page reviews were much too long to be of general interest. Therefore, we condensed the reviews and placed details in appendixes. Concurrently, we formulated and reformulated our theoretical ideas about the creative person and the creative process.

In the first chapter of this book we explain our focus on real-life creativity and discuss several related issues, such as the characteristics of a creative product and the two levels of creativity. Chapter 2 reviews the evidence for the validity of a wide variety of tests as measures of creativity in science and science-related fields. This review demonstrates the lack of such validity for most widely used creativity tests. Our theories on the personal characteristics necessary for creativity in science are presented in chapter 3. We use these characteristics to develop a multidimensional theory of creativity in scientists.

Chapter 4 reviews the evidence linking family and child-rearing antecedents to creativity. In chapter 5, we present a theory of the creative process in science. Finally, in chapter 6, we review our principal conclusions and integrate our theorizing about child-rearing antecedents, personal characteristics, and the creative process into a unified model.

We would like to thank Wayne Maxson of Paley Library at Temple University for his help in obtaining a number of obscure publications. We also thank Drs. Helmut Bartel, Joseph DuCette, and Daniel Solomon for their valuable comments on earlier drafts of this manuscript. Finally, we gratefully acknowledge a research leave granted to the second author by Temple University.

Creativity in Science: An Introduction

ACCORDING TO A POPULAR STEREOTYPE, the scientist is rational, unemotional, detached, and dedicated solely to the pursuit of truth. In his work, he uses the scientific method—deducing hypotheses from theory, testing the hypotheses systematically, and revising the theory as necessary. This stereotype is not totally false; but, for many scientists, especially the most creative ones, it is inappropriate. For example, B. F. Skinner (1959), the well-known psychologist, has denied that his own work proceeded according to *the* scientific method:

> The notes, data, and publications which I have examined do not show that I ever behaved in the manner of Man Thinking as described by John Stuart Mill or John Dewey or as in reconstructions of scientific behavior by other philosophers of science. I never faced a problem which was more than the eternal problem of finding order. I never attacked a problem by constructing a Hypothesis. I never deduced Theorems or submitted them to Exper-

imental Check. So far as I can see, I had no preconceived Model of behavior—certainly not a physiological or mentalistic one, and I believe, not a conceptual one. . . . Of course, I was working on a basic Assumption—that there was order in behavior if I could only discover it—but such an assumption is not to be confused with the hypotheses of deductive theory. It is also true that I exercised a certain Selection of Facts, but not because of relevance to theory but because one fact was more orderly than another. If I engaged in Experimental Design at all, it was simply to complete or extend some evidence of order already observed. (P. 369)

The scientific method also seems inadequate as a description of Darwin's work. Howard Gruber (1974), who analyzed many of Darwin's notebooks, commented:

The picture of scientific thought is often painted as being carried forward by the construction of alternative hypotheses followed by the rational choice between them. Darwin's notebooks do not support this rationalist myth. Hypotheses are discovered with difficulty in the activity of a person holding *one* point of view, and they are the expression of that point of view. It is hard enough to have one reasonable hypothesis, and two at a time may be exceedingly rare. In Darwin's case, when he is forced to give up one hypothesis, he does not necessarily substitute another—he sometimes simply remains at a loss until his point of view matures sufficiently to permit the expression of a new hypothesis. (P. 146)

The belief that scientists are detached, rational, and dedicated solely to the pursuit of truth has also been challenged. James Watson (1968), in his account of the discovery of the structure of DNA, depicts some less noble characteristics in himself and some of his colleagues: competitiveness, arrogance, even deviousness.

Unlike the general public, most scientists probably believe the popular stereotypes about scientists are mistaken. But what are scientists really like, and how do they go about their work? Much research, theory, and speculation have been addressed to these questions by scholars in a variety of fields. For example, sociologists have studied the effects of different work settings on the creativity of scientists. And educators have been interested in the training of scientists. However, these are not topics of primary interest in this book. Our focus is on creative scientists and the characteristics and processes that set them apart from less creative scientists.

What do we mean by creative scientists? In psychology, defining creativity has been a perplexing problem, which we will consider shortly. For the moment, we shall define creative scientists as those whose work is considered high in both originality and value by other scientists in the same field.

Although creativity has been actively studied by psychologists for many years, there are relatively few studies on creative scientists and only a small number on scientists within any specific field or domain. However, there was no compelling reason to expect that the characteristics and processes associated with creativity would differ across scientific fields. Therefore, in considering evidence for inclusion in this book, we have defined science broadly, so as to include both the natural and social sciences. Because of the sparsity of research on creative scientists, we have also considered evidence from some other fields, such as mathematics, architecture, and engineering, which have generated research on creativity but are not usually considered sciences. Throughout the book, we have tried to avoid generalizations based on evidence from a single scientific field.

We will be concerned primarily with the psychology of creative scientists—the abilities, personal characteristics, motives, and processes that set these scientists apart from other scientists. Since these are psychological concerns, we shall begin by describing two basic approaches that psychologists have used to study creativity.

Researchers using the first approach define creativity by test performance. The tests most commonly used for this purpose are those developed by Guilford (1967b; Guilford and Hoepfner, 1971), Torrance (1966), and others to measure divergent thinking abilities. Divergent thinking is needed when there are many possible answers or solutions to a problem. For example, one type of problem found on many divergent thinking tests requires a person to think of many different and unusual uses for a common item, such as a tin can or a brick. It is often assumed that the abilities used to solve such problems are also essential to real-life creative endeavors. It does not matter for our purposes which ability or trait the test is designed to measure. What does matter is that the researcher begins with a priori assumptions about creative persons or their processes. One general strategy of these researchers is to search for correlates of the creativity test scores in other ability and personality tests. For example, Wallach and Kogan (1965), in their well-known study, related creativity test scores to measures of such factors as intelligence, academic achievement, conceptual style, anxiety, and defensiveness. Another strategy has been to try to influence creativity test scores by experimentally manipulating instructions or situational factors or by providing training in creative thinking skills. Studies of the effectiveness of these attempts have been reviewed by Mansfield, Busse, and Krepelka (1978) and by Stein (1974, 1975).

Such studies may provide interesting results, but they cannot tell us much about real-life creativity. As Wallach (1971) has argued, creativity test scores do not vary one-to-one with creative attainments, and they can be expected to show individual differences for reasons that have nothing to do with real-life creativity. For example, a person can get a higher score on a tin-can uses test if eagerness to please the tester causes him to use extra effort in generating alternatives. In chapter 2, we show that, for scientists, most divergent thinking tests do not correlate at all with measures of real-life creativity. Even among the few tests that do show positive correlations, none approximates a one-to-one relationship. Thus the first approach to creativity, defining it in terms of test performance, will not help us to understand real-life creativity in science.

The second and more promising approach is to measure real-life creativity and relate it to other variables, such as personality characteristics and child-rearing experiences (e.g., Wallach, 1976). But measuring real-life creativity presents a conceptual problem: before we can measure it, we must have some notion of what it is. Real-life creativity is shown in products such as essays, books, paintings, inventions, patents, and research articles. But exactly what characteristics make a product creative?

First, the product must be novel or unusual in relation to other products. Novelty alone, however, is an insufficient criterion: the suggestion that automobile windshields be made from cellophane is novel; but it would not be judged creative, because it is unworkable. A creative product must possess some value or appropriateness in addition to novelty.

Novelty and value are the criteria most commonly used to define creative products, but some psychologists have suggested that additional criteria are needed to identify products exceptionally high in creativity. Jackson and Messick (1967), for example, suggest criteria of transformation and condensation. They define transformation as follows:

> One property present in some products but absent, or less obvious, in others is the power to transform the constraints of reality. Some objects combine elements in ways that defy tradition and that yield a new perspective. They literally force us to see reality in a new way. These products involve a *transformation* of material or ideas to overcome conventional constraints. (P. 6)

Condensation, according to Jackson and Messick, is a characteristic of the most highly creative accomplishments of man:

> Products that warrant close and repeated examination
> are those that do not divulge their total meaning on first
> viewing. These products offer something new each time
> we experience them, whether they are great works of art
> or highly developed scientific theories. They have about
> them an intensity and a concentration of meaning re-
> quiring continued contemplation. (Pp. 10–11)

All the criteria for creativity in a product—novelty, value, transformation, and condensation—involve relative judgments. For example, what is novel in a field depends on what has already been produced: in the 1860s, the impressionist style of painting was considered highly novel, but the use of this style today is not. The degree of novelty also depends on the reference group with which a creator is compared: a high school student's science fair project may be highly creative in relation to other student projects, but not when compared to the products of research scientists.

Although we can identify the abstract criteria for creative products, there remains the problem of operationally defining and measuring real-life creativity. An obvious solution would be to have experts rate the products for creativity. But, perhaps because researchers have been more interested in the creativity of persons than of individual products, this approach has seldom been used. Creativity is probably better appreciated in a series of products than in any single piece of work, yet obtaining separate ratings for a large sample of an individual's products is expensive and time-consuming; thus researchers have usually measured real-life creativity with ratings of persons. We believe these ratings are likely to possess validity when the criteria for creativity are carefully specified and the raters have expertise in the areas of the persons being rated. Creativity ratings of persons can, of course, be contaminated by factors such as productivity, popularity, and professional visibility. These and other problems associated with the use of ratings are discussed in chapter 2.

A new approach to measuring real-life creativity is available for use in scientific fields. *Science Citation Index* contains data on the number of times a scientist's work is cited by other scientists. Since scientists presumably cite work they judge to be original and valuable, citation counts offer promise as measures of creativity. Further discussion of citation counts can be found in chapter 2.

TWO LEVELS OF CREATIVITY

Earlier, we proposed that creativity is a relative concept. Products can be considered creative only in relation to other products at a particular point in time. Thus, the creativity of any product depends on the reference group of products to which it is being compared. These reference groups, of course, change over the years, and different reference groups can be used to identify different levels of creativity.

We, along with others (e.g., Arieti, 1976), believe it is useful to distinguish between two broad levels of creativity. The higher level is defined by a reference group of professionals in the field, and the lower level by reference groups other than the professional one. Products judged creative at the professional level constitute significant advances in their fields. The same cannot usually be said of products judged creative at a sub-professional level.

Although we use these reference groups to define two levels of creativity, it should be understood that the levels could also be defined using the criteria for creative products—novelty, value, transformation, and condensation. For example, a higher-level product might be identified on the basis of a high degree of transformation. But, in research, it is in some ways more useful to define operationally the reference groups than to define the criteria for creative products.

The English language lacks a word for creativity at the professional level. Such a word is badly needed in view of the looseness with which the term *creativity* is currently applied. Accordingly, we have used the adjective *auctorive,* borrowed from the Latin *auctor,* to refer to creativity at the professional level. *Auctor* has had a variety of meanings in Latin; among these are "maker," "builder," "author," and "inventor." We shall use the term *auctor* to refer to a person who has demonstrated creativity at the professional level.

Einstein, Rutherford, Mozart, and Picasso were obviously auctors. But thousands of other professionals unknown outside of their fields are also auctors, because they have made significant, innovative contributions to their areas of specialization. Clearly, there is a wide range of creativity within the auctorive level. A scientist may be considered an auctor because his invention of a new steering mechanism for automobiles is a valuable innovation, but he would not be considered as creative as a Nobel prize winner. We believe that, within the auctorive level, products embodying the highest levels of transformation are the most creative. Such products necessarily show novelty, and many also show condensation.

Below the auctorive level of creativity is a second broad level, which we call *amateur creativity.* Persons judged creative at the amateur level would not ordinarily be considered creative at the auctorive level. But amateur creatives do show creativity in comparison to their nonprofessional peers. Among the ranks of amateur creatives are high school science fair winners, sixth-graders whose essays are considered unusually creative by their teachers, and amateur photographers whose pictures are awarded prizes at their school or college. There is a continuum of creativity within the amateur level, just as there is within the auctorive level. But amateur creativity is much more common than auctorive creativity; many people show some evidence of amateur creativity.

In studying scientific creativity, we have focused upon the auctorive level. Auctorive products, unlike most amateur products, are valuable to science and often to society. Most research on scientific creativity has been done with scientists at the lower end of the auctorive level. For example, industrial researchers working in a large firm are rated for creativity, and scientists judged high in creativity are compared with scientists judged lower. There are a few studies, however, that compare eminent scientists with other scientists drawn randomly from professional directories, and most of what we know about the creative process in science comes from personal accounts by highly creative auctors, such as Charles Darwin.

Although we are primarily concerned with auctors, we shall occasionally consider research on amateur creatives, usually high school or college students. It seems reasonable to assume that most auctors in science emerge from the ranks of amateur creatives. There have been no longitudinal studies to verify this assumption, although studies by Ypma (1968) and Parloff, Datta, Kleman, and Handlon (1968) provide supportive evidence. Ypma found that industrial research scientists who reported having conducted a scientific experiment on their own initiative in both high school and college were judged to be more creative in their professional work than those who had not. He also found that the more creative scientists were more likely to report having built an original apparatus on their own initiative in college. Parloff et al. found that the personality structure of auctors in four fields was similar to the personality structure of high school males who entered a national science competition and who also scored at least at the eightieth percentile on a science aptitude examination. More research is needed to determine under what conditions amateur creatives develop into auctors.

Problems in Studying Auctorive Creativity

Our goal throughout this book is to present a view of highly creative scientists: their personal characteristics, their formative experiences, and the processes they use in their work. This approach entails few theoretical pre-conceptions about auctorive creativity. We do not assume, for example, that special mental abilities are essential to creativity. We do not even assume, a priori, that there are common characteristics to be found in auctors from different fields.

Our approach has limitations. Studies of auctors are only as good as the means used to identify them. Furthermore, since most of the relevant studies deal with those who have already made auctorive contributions, it is not clear whether their characteristics are antecedents or consequents of their auctorive success. For example, if auctorive scientists show a high level of personal autonomy, we cannot be certain whether the autonomy antedated the creative accomplishments, whether it was the result of such accomplishments, or whether some interactive process was at work. Childhood personality data for auctors and comparison scientists might help us to select among these alternatives. But few such data are available. Despite the limitations, however, we believe that there is enough consistent evidence to permit some tentative conclusions.

2

Test Performance and Creativity in Science

THE DIVERSITY OF THEORIES of creativity is mirrored by the diversity of tests designed to measure creativity. Over the past thirty years, dozens of measures have been developed to assess creativity and its hypothesized components, such as originality and flexibility. This very diversity of measures reflects a fundamental weakness in the literature: most creativity measures have been constructed and subsequently selected for use because they seem to tap at least a part of what common sense points to as creativity. Yet most investigators have paid scant attention to the validity of the measures they use.

Our primary purpose in this chapter is to review the best available evidence of the validity of various tests as measures of creativity in science. A secondary purpose is to review the studies relating scientific creativity to test performance in general; this research provides good evidence about the characteristics of creative persons. Both purposes are served by examining the relationship of various tests to real-life creativity in science. These tests will include ones traditionally labeled "creativity tests" as well as a broad spectrum of other measures.

First, let us consider the methodological problems involved in establishing validity for any creativity test. These include a consideration of the applicability of different types of validity to creativity and a brief discussion of the value of various creativity criteria.

PROBLEMS IN THE VALIDATION STUDIES: INADEQUACY OF MOST TYPES OF VALIDITY

There are several approaches to validating creativity tests, but we believe strong evidence for the validity of a test can be established only through criterion-related validity studies that relate test performance to real-life creative accomplishments. Other approaches to validation, such as establishing content validity or construct validity, have serious limitations when applied to creativity.

To establish content validity, for example, one must demonstrate that a test samples some domain in a representative way. But, since there is little agreement on what creativity is or what it encompasses, it seems impossible to establish content validity for measures of creativity.

To establish construct validity, one must show that a measure taps a theoretical construct and is related to other variables according to predictions based on the theoretical construct. Moreover, researchers must be in general agreement on the predicted relations among the variables in question (Cronbach and Meehl, 1955). But since researchers have different conceptions of creativity (e.g., Getzels, 1975; Treffinger, Renzulli, and Feldhusen, 1971; Yamamoto, 1965), they often do not agree on the predicted relationships of creativity to other variables.

For example, theorists in the Gestalt tradition emphasize convergent, problem-solving processes in creativity, whereas associationist theorists emphasize divergent thinking processes (Busse & Mansfield, 1980). An associationist theorist might try to validate a divergent thinking test by correlating it with a personality scale that measures openness to experience, since a person with a broad range of experiences would have a large pool of ideas and potential associations to use in divergent thinking tasks. But demonstrating a positive correlation between these measures would not convince a Gestalt theorist of the validity of the divergent thinking test, because Gestalt theorists do not believe that divergent thinking is central to creativity in the first place. Hence, the usefulness of construct validity is questionable when applied to creativity tests.[1]

Another common approach to validity is validation of a measure through comparison with established measures. But it cannot be used because there is no creativity measure with accepted and proven validity.

Criterion Measures of Creativity

Criterion-related validity studies offer the best hope for validating creativity tests, but even these studies are not without problems. One of the most serious problems concerns the selection of an appropriate real-life criterion measure.

Since, in chapter 1, we defined creativity in terms of products, it might seem the most desirable measure of scientific creativity would be anonymous ratings by experts of products such as articles, books, and patents. But this approach has seldom been used with scientists. One reason is that scientists and their products are likely to be known to experts in a field. And it is, of

---

1. We are using construct validity in its conventional, restricted sense. The term has sometimes been used to embrace all possible validation strategies (Anastasi, 1976, p. 159).

course, more economical and efficient simply to rate the persons.

The criteria most often used in criterion-related validity studies of creativity tests are various forms of ratings. Problems inherent in the use of various creativity criteria have been discussed extensively by Brogden and Sprecher (1964), Christie (1970), Harmon (1963), Rossman and Gollob (1975), Thorndike (1966), Treffinger, Renzulli, and Feldhusen (1971), and Yamamoto (1965). More general limitations related to the reliability and validity of criteria are discussed in Cronbach (1971), Lent, Aurbach, and Levin (1971), and Schmidt, Hunter, and Urry (1976). Most of the ratings used in the studies reviewed here are of three types: (1) supervisory ratings; (2) expert ratings by personally known colleagues; or (3) expert ratings by colleagues in the scientific community.

Supervisory ratings are subject to halo effects which may occur because administrators are accustomed to looking for characteristics other than creativity, such as productivity, efficiency, intelligence, and socio-emotional qualities (e.g., Bennett, 1969). But supervisors who are familiar with an individual's work and who are knowledgeable in the appropriate specialization should be capable of producing ratings that are reasonably valid.

Expert ratings by personally known colleagues are potentially subject to halo effects resulting from friendships and other socio-emotional factors. Perceptions of intelligence or productivity may also contaminate the ratings. But, as is the case for supervisors, if the experts are familiar with an individual's work and knowledgeable in the area of specialization, they should be capable of producing reasonably valid ratings.

Expert ratings by colleagues in the scientific community have been used to identify distinguished scientists within a field (Chambers, 1964; Clark, 1957; Roe, 1951a, 1951b, 1953). Groups of "eminent," "outstanding," or "creative" men are chosen by some combination of awards, honors, and ratings by experts in a field. This approach, although promising, is not without limitations. The selected scientists can obtain high ratings by political as well as scholarly accomplishments. For example, election to office in professional associations may substantially influence these ratings. Whether these political influences are explicit (e.g., Clark, 1957) or implicit (e.g., Chambers, 1964), they are almost certainly a factor in the ratings. One way to reduce political influence on ratings would be to insure that raters and ratees come from the same subspecialty. For example, developmental psychologists would rate only other developmental psychologists; social psychologists would rate only other social psychologists; and so forth. The importance of such a procedure becomes self-evident when one considers the dilemma faced by an individual attempting to rate the creativity of persons whose research and scholarship are unknown to him. He may decline to rate or rate on the basis of visibility or general reputation. Insuring that raters and ratees come from the same subspecialty would eliminate any bias that raters might have toward persons in other subspecialties and would increase the likelihood that ratings would be based on informed judgments of professional work. However, political influence on the ratings would not be completely eliminated.

In addition to the ratings criteria just considered, another exceptionally promising criterion deserves mention: the number of citations to published work. The *Science Citation Index* provides data on the number of citations each year to virtually all scientific articles and books in the English language. The *Social Science Citation Index* provides similar data for the social sciences. The number of citations is one indicator of the extent to which a scientist's work has influenced other scientists.

Citation counts are conceptually separable from productivity. A scientist who, in a three-year period, publishes only a single seminal article may nevertheless receive hundreds of citations, whereas another scientist who publishes dozens of articles in the same time period may receive only a handful of citations. (Of course, such a possibility is unlikely.) Citation counts seem to be minimally influenced by area of specialization (Cole and Cole, 1971). Citation counts have been used extensively by researchers in the sociology of science (e.g., Bayer and Folger, 1966; Cole, 1970; Cole and Cole, 1972; Lindsey, 1976; Reskin, 1977; White and White, 1977) but only rarely by psychologists studying creativity. The availability of citation counts opens up many new possibilities for research on scientific creativity.

Differentiating Creativity
Criteria from Related Variables

If creativity is to prove useful as a concept, it must be conceptually differentiated from related, potentially contaminating variables such as productivity, general reputation or visibility, quality of work, and quantity of work. But, from a theoretical standpoint, creativity criteria need not show complete independence, since the generation of creative products generally augments the related variables.

Empirical distinctions between the concepts of creativity, productivity, general reputation or visibility, quality of work, and quantity of work sometimes have been cloudy, even if reasonable theoretical distinctions can be made. Donald Taylor (1963, pp. 231–33), in a study of about one hundred male electronics personnel, found correlations of about .60 between supervisors' ratings of creativity and their ratings of productivity. Fifty-nine of these men were later rated by immediate supervisors on quality of work, quantity of work, originality, and initiative. Intercorrelations ranged from .39 to .69.

A similar result was obtained by Donald MacKinnon (1964, p. 363) in an analysis of forty architects rated relatively high on creativity. The correlation between their creativity ratings by editors of architectural journals and their number of articles published was .59. The architects' ratings of their own creativity correlated .50 with the number of articles.

Cole and Cole (1967), studying 120 physicists, found the total number of published papers correlated .60 with the total number of citations and .72 with a weighted citation index that the Coles used as a measure of quality. They also found the physicists' scope of reputation correlated .63 with their quality index. Stanley and Thomasson (1957) found a correlation of .49 between peer ratings of creativity and the number of publications in two leading measurement journals for twenty-five prominent psychometricians. However, they found a correlation of only .12 between creativity and *total* number of publications. These and other studies (Blume and Sinclair, 1973; Clark, 1957; Dennis, 1954; Meltzer, 1949) suggest that moderate correlations are to be expected between such variables as creativity, productivity, and general reputation.

Other researchers have presented additional evidence that creativity criteria are distinguishable from related dimensions. Calvin Taylor and his associates (Taylor, Smith, and Ghiselin, 1960, 1963) collected a diverse sample of fifty-six criteria for 166 scientists from various disciplines in an attempt to clarify the interrelationships of various criteria. Taylor and his associates factor-analyzed fifty-two of these criteria and located fifteen factors, one of which they entitled "originality of written work." Other factors were found which represented productivity, visibility, quality of work, and quantity of work. Mullins (1959), using 131 research physical scientists, found an insignificant correlation between a composite supervisors' creativity rating and the total number of published articles. Sprecher (1959), studying 107 male engineers in a large industrial organization, found that peer and supervisory ratings of creativity correlated .64 and that each correlated with number of patent disclosures about

.30. Thus, despite evidence of moderate positive correlations between creativity, productivity, and visibility, there is evidence that these criteria are separable.[2]

Problems with Research Design and Statistics

The make-up of the control group has vexed investigators studying high-level professional creativity. In some studies, control groups seem particularly inadequate. For example, when "creatives" in one field are compared with "noncreatives" in a different field or with the general population (e.g., Cross, Cattell, and Butcher, 1967; Drevdahl and Cattell, 1958; Myden, 1959; Raychaudhuri, 1971; Stuteville, 1966), field differences are confounded with creativity differences. But in other studies, the inadequacy of a control group is less easily detected. For example, studies which compare eminent or creative psychologists with a sample of other psychologists may confound specialization differences with creativity. Control group members may come largely from specializations such as clinical psychology, where relatively few persons do research, whereas creative group members may come predominantly from specializations such as experimental psychology, in which most do research. One way of coping with this problem is to restrict voting to specified subgroups (e.g., Clark, 1957).

A related problem occurs when different measurement procedures are used for the creative and the comparison groups. This occurs, for example, when some or all members of the creative groups are tested in person and control group members are tested by mail (e.g., Barron, 1968, 1969; Helson and Crutchfield, 1970; MacKinnon, 1962a, 1962b). Such differences in test administration affect findings to an unknown degree.

---

2. For a thorough discussion of several issues raised here, see Cole and Cole, 1973, pp. 21–36.

Another limitation occurs in statistical analyses: almost without exception only linear relationships between the criteria and other measures have been considered. But the existence of curvilinear relationships is at least plausible, particularly between creativity criteria and personality variables. Consider, for example, a variable such as psychological autonomy. Without a fairly high level of autonomy, it seems unlikely that a person could develop products that represent a transformation of existing artistic, literary, or scientific conventions. Yet an extreme level of autonomy could prove inimical to creative accomplishments, since a minimal level of cooperation with others is necessary to maintain a job. A moderately high level of autonomy is probably optimal for the development of creative products.

A final methodological limitation needs to be mentioned. Researchers in the field of creativity may sometimes report only partial results (e.g., Barron, 1961, 1966, 1968; Gough, 1961, 1975). They may give dozens of tests yielding hundreds of subscores but then emphasize only the findings that seem most promising. Capitalization on chance occurs, to an often unknown degree. Moreover, the published validity research is probably a nonrandom sample of the actual work done, since nonsignificant results are less likely to be published.

SELECTION CRITERIA

The methodological concerns detailed in the previous section led to the following criteria for use in the selection of studies for this review:

1. Validity had to be established using adults. No studies using students at any level (elementary, secondary, college, graduate, or military training) were included. Because students are still learning their profession, they are unlikely, by themselves, to produce works comparable in either originality or value to those of professionals in the field.

2. The creativity criterion could consist of ratings by

supervisors, colleagues, or experts in the area. Alternatively, an objective criterion, such as the number of patents, could be used. The criterion had to be conceptually separable from productivity, visibility, and technical expertise.

3. Comparisons of creative and less creative subjects had to be made within the same field; otherwise creativity differences could easily be confounded with field differences.

4. The subjects had to be in science or a science-related field.

5. The measures had to be completed by the subjects themselves. Results from creativity ratings by psychologists and measures completed by psychologists about other persons were not included.

Many of the measures reviewed here are not usually considered creativity measures. But such considerations are somewhat arbitrary, given the state of creativity research (e.g., Crockenberg, 1972). Therefore, no a priori decisions were made about which tests to review. If two criterion-related validity studies of adult creative performance, both using a particular measure, could be located, the measure was included for review. Occasionally, a measure was included because it was used in a single study of particular merit.

One final consideration is relevant to the scope of this review. When identical or highly overlapping results of the same study are presented in more than one place, only a single key reference is generally cited.

The review is divided into three sections: (1) cognitive and perceptual tests; (2) personality, vocational, and miscellaneous tests; and (3) personal history questionnaires. In order to simplify the presentation of a large body of information, we shall discuss in this chapter only those tests with *positive evidence* for criterion-related validity in scientific and related fields. The evidence bearing on the validity of the remaining tests meeting our criteria is reviewed in appendixes A and B.

References for the tests themselves are cited only where standard references are insufficient. Most measures can be traced through standard sources (Buros, 1959, 1965, 1972, 1978; Davis, 1971; French, Ekstrom, and Price, 1963; Guilford and Hoepfner, 1971; Kaltsounis, 1971, 1972).

COGNITIVE AND PERCEPTUAL TESTS

A vast number of cognitive and perceptual tests have been used in research on creativity. But for many tests, no studies could be located which attempted to establish criterion-related validity with adults in scientific and related fields. The four tests showing some promise as measures of creative accomplishments in science are marked with an asterisk. These tests are described in this chapter and studies relating them to scientific creativity are briefly summarized. The remaining tests are discussed in appendix A. Studies that met our selection criteria were located for the following tests:

* AC Test of Creative Ability
  Apparatus Test
  Concept Mastery Test
  Consequences Test
  Gestalt Completion Test
  Gestalt Transformation Test
  Gottschaldt Figures Test
  Ideational Fluency Test
  Match Problems Test
  Pertinent Questions Test
* Plot Titles Test
* Remote Associates Test
  Social Institutions Test
* Test for Selecting Research Personnel
  Unusual Uses Tests
  Wechsler Adult Intelligence Scale
  Word Association Tests

Throughout this section, all subscales that showed significant relationships with the creativity criteria will be noted. The remaining subscales mentioned by the researchers showed nonsignificant relationships.

AC Test of Creative Ability

This test is designed to measure the quantity and uniqueness of ideas. There are five subtests: (1) common situations; (2) general reasoning; (3) sensitivity to problems; (4) practical judgment; and (5) originality. A short form (AC Spark Plug Division, 1959), consisting of subtests 1, 2, and 5, is often used.

The AC test has been scored in a variety of ways. The types of scores include: (1) a quantity score, which is the total number of relevant responses listed; (2) a uniqueness score, which reflects the unusualness of responses as compared with responses generally given; (3) a quality score, which reflects the speed and economy of proposed solutions; and (4) a total score which is a weighted combination of quantity and uniqueness scores. The short form of the test is usually scored only for quantity.

Goodman, Furcon, and Rose (1969), using sixty-three research scientists and engineers, found a nonsignificant correlation of .08 between supervisors' ratings of ideational fluency and the number of acceptable responses made to the AC Test of Creative Ability.

Harris (1955), who developed the AC test, reported several studies using all five subtests. One study used eighteen persons from engineering and related fields who were selected by their supervisors for outstanding performance according to Harris' working definition of creativity and eighteen who were similarly selected for weak performance. The creative persons scored significantly higher on the total score and on seven of eight subscores. In another study, Harris compared twenty-two engineers rated as satisfactory performers on creative tasks and thirteen rated as occasionally unsatisfactory. The satisfactory group scored significantly higher on the total score of the AC test and on all eight subtest scores. In two additional studies, involving thirty-two and twenty-four engineers respectively, the only score obtained—the quantity score—was significantly related to supervisors' ratings of creative performance.

In summary, a series of studies by Harris found the AC Test of Creative Ability to be related to creative engineering performance, but one other study did not.

Plot Titles Test

This test requires a subject to write titles for short-story plots. The test is typically scored for the number of clever titles listed and for the number of not-clever titles. Sometimes the total number of titles listed is also scored.

Mullins (1959) used the Plot Titles Test with 131 research scientists. The test was scored for clever responses, not-clever responses, and total responses. Only the clever responses score was significantly correlated with supervisors' ratings of creativity.

Sprecher (1957) administered his version of the Plot Titles Test to 107 male engineers. Peer rankings, but not supervisory rankings, of creativity showed low correlations with the clever responses score. Neither ranking was related to the not-clever responses score.

Walker (1955) scored the Plot Titles Test for the number of clever titles listed. No differences were found between eighteen highly creative chemists and mathematicians and twelve other chemists and mathematicians. The creatives in each field were identified by expert peers.

To summarize, the clever responses score of the Plot Titles Test shows some promise in measuring creativity. The not-clever responses score seems unrelated to creativity.

Remote Associates Test

The Remote Associates Test (RAT) was developed by Sarnoff Mednick (Mednick and Mednick, 1967). Each of the thirty items on the form for adults contains three words; the subject must find a fourth word which is related to all three.

Datta (1964a) found a nonsignificant relationship between scores on the RAT and supervisors' creativity ratings for thirty-one physicists. However, the findings may be misleading, since, as Datta noted, ten of the physicists did not speak English, the language of the test, as their native language. In a second study, using the RAT with twenty-one engineers, Datta (1964b) again found no significant correlation with supervisors' ratings of creativity.

Goodman, Furcon, and Rose (1969), in a study of sixty-three research scientists and engineers, found a significant positive correlation of .27 between RAT scores and supervisors' ratings of the subjects' remote association ability, which was defined as the ability to combine elements into new and useful combinations.

Two studies by Gordon (Gordon, 1972; Mednick and Mednick, 1967) showed relationships of the RAT to industrial research performance. In the first study, involving thirty-seven industrial research scientists and engineers, high scorers on the RAT wrote significantly more proposals and were awarded significantly more research contracts than low scorers. In the second study, using twenty-nine chemists, high scorers made significantly more patent disclosures and applications and obtained significantly more patents than did low scorers.

Mednick and Mednick (1967) reported a study by Chiranian involving an unspecified number of research scientists. RAT scores were unrelated to supervisors' judgments of the scientists' creativity; however, the number of research proposals submitted and the number of research contracts won by these scientists were significantly related to RAT performance.

Pelz and Andrews (1976) gave the RAT to 355 scientists and engineers. On the basis of education and position, these subjects were divided into five groups. Senior persons from both supervisory and nonsupervisory levels rated each subject's contribution to general technical or scientific knowledge in the field over the preceding five years. These ratings were not significantly correlated with RAT scores for any of the five groups. Many secondary analyses were carried out, but their meaning is unclear.

On balance, the RAT shows limited promise as a measure of creativity. When supervisors' ratings of creativity were used, no significant relationships with creativity criteria were found. Criteria such as number of research proposals submitted and number of research contracts won have shown relationships to RAT performance; but these latter criteria may be more related to conventional intelligence than to creativity. The relationships of these criteria to RAT performance are probably due partly to the verbal ability component of the RAT and partly to that portion of the RAT variance which is independent of general intelligence. Wallach (1970, p. 1246) reports correlations averaging about .40 between the RAT and verbal ability tests of intelligence. But, as Wallach (1970) and Mendelsohn (1976) point out, the verbal ability component of the RAT cannot completely explain the observed link between the RAT and real-life creativity. Both Wallach and Mendelsohn believe that an attentional processes component in the RAT is also necessary to account for this link.

Test for Selecting Research Personnel

This test (American Institute for Research, 1954) consists of 150 multiple-choice items, each of which presents the subject with a problem aimed at one of the critical requirements for scientific research personnel. The subject must select from five alternatives the one which best solves the problem. The three sections of the test tap three sets of abilities regarded as important in research: (1) formulating problems and hypotheses and planning and designing investigations; (2) conducting investigations and interpreting research results; (3) preparing reports, administering research, and accepting organizational and personal responsibility. One year of college education in physics, chemistry, and mathematics is assumed for the test. Examination of the content of the items suggests that the test may tap the reasoning abilities that are measured in IQ tests.

Donald Taylor (1963) found the total score from this test correlated significantly with supervisory ratings of originality in a sample of sixty-six male physicists. Taylor also found the three subscores, as well as the total score, were significantly related to creativity ratings by immediate supervisors for another sample of about one hundred male electronics engineers and scientists. These two studies indicate that the test has promise as a measure of scientific creativity.

PERSONALITY, VOCATIONAL, AND MISCELLANEOUS TESTS

A large variety of noncognitive tests have occasionally been used to predict creativity criteria. However, only fifteen of these tests met the criteria for inclusion in this review. These tests are listed below. The seven tests showing some promise as measures of creative accomplishments in science are marked with asterisks. These tests are described in this chapter, and studies relating them to scientific creativity are briefly summarized. The other tests are reviewed in Appendix B.

* Adjective Check List
* Barron-Welsh Art Scale
* California Psychological Inventory
  Chapin Social Insight Test
  Kuder Preference Record (Vocational)
  Manifest Anxiety Scale
  Mechanical Comprehension Test
  Minnesota Multiphasic Personality Inventory
* Mosaic Construction Test
  Motivation Analysis Test
  Myers-Briggs Type Indicator

* Self-Description Inventory (Initiative Scale)
* Sixteen Personality Factor Questionnaire
* Strong Vocational Interest Blank
  Study of Values

Throughout this section, all subscales which showed significant relationships with creativity criteria will be noted. The remaining subscales mentioned by the researchers showed nonsignificant relationships.

Adjective Check List

The Adjective Check List consists of 300 adjectives. A subject checks the ones he considers to be self-descriptive. When the Gough and Heilbrun (1965) keys are used, the measure yields twenty-four scores: number of adjectives checked, defensiveness, favorable adjectives checked, unfavorable adjectives checked, self-confidence, self-control, lability (the tendency to be easily moved or changed, not rigid, free in the expression of emotion), personal adjustment, achievement, dominance, endurance, order, intraception, (the tendency to engage in attempts to understand one's own behavior or the behavior of others), nurturance, affiliation, heterosexuality, exhibition, autonomy, aggression, change, succorance (the tendency to solicit sympathy, affection, or emotional support from others), abasement, deference, and counseling readiness.

Helson and Crutchfield (1970) studied twenty-seven to thirty-four creative and twenty-nine comparison male mathematicians. Creativity was rated by other mathematicians. The only significant finding for the Adjective Check List was that the creative mathematicians scored higher than the comparison group on the lability scale.

MacKinnon (1963), studying 124 male architects, reported that creativity as rated by architectural experts showed significant positive correlations with the following scores from the Adjective Check List: aggression, autonomy, change, exhibition, lability, and number of unfavorable adjectives. The creativity ratings showed significant negative correlations with scales measuring abasement, affiliation, defensiveness, deference, endurance, heterosexuality, intraception, nurturance, order, personal adjustment, and self-control.

McDermid (1965) gave the Adjective Check List to fifty-eight male engineers and technical personnel. Using twenty-one of the Gough and Heilbrun scales, he found the deference scale correlated negatively and the autonomy scale correlated positively with peer evaluations of creativity. Supervisory creativity ratings were negatively related to the heterosexuality scale.

Despite the diversity of populations studied with the Adjective Check List, some patterns of consistency emerged. The autonomy and lability scales tended to show evidence of a positive relationship with creativity; the deference and heterosexuality scales showed evidence of a negative relationship.

Barron-Welsh Art Scale

This test, developed by Barron and Welsh (1952), consists of eighty-six line drawings, most of which are more or less abstract. The drawings vary from simple and symmetrical to complex and asymmetrical. Subjects are required to indicate which drawings they like. Sixty-two of these items are scored for the Barron-Welsh Art Scale. A slightly different variation of the Barron-Welsh Art Scale, called the Revised Art Scale, has also been developed. This revised scale consists of thirty drawings that artists like more frequently than most people and thirty drawings that artists dislike more often than most people (Welsh, 1975, pp. 62–63). The two scales are highly correlated (Welsh, 1975, p. 63). A high score on either scale indicates a preference for complex and asymmetrical drawings.

In one study, Gough (1961) tested forty-five industrial research scientists. The Barron-Welsh Art Scale showed a significant correlation of .41 with a creativity criterion consisting of combined peer and supervisory creativity ratings. This correlation was higher than that obtained for any of the more than one hundred other test and questionnaire variables he used in this study.

Helson (1971) tested about forty-five female mathematicians and found that a creative group did not differ significantly from a comparison group of female mathematicians on the Barron-Welsh Art Scale. The groups were established on the basis of ratings by expert mathematicians.

The Barron-Welsh Art Scale was also used by Helson and Crutchfield (1970) in a similar study of about sixty male mathematicians. Mathematicians rated creative by experts scored significantly higher on the Art Scale than did a comparison group of mathematicians.

MacKinnon (1961, 1965) administered the Barron-Welsh Art Scale to forty male architects rated creative by architectural experts and to about the same number of other architects in each of two comparison groups. Creative architects showed a significantly greater preference for complex and asymmetrical drawings than the members of a comparison group consisting of architects who had never worked with any of the creative architects. Apparently no differences were found between the preferences of creative architects and those of a second comparison group, which consisted of architects who had had at least two years of work experience with the creative architects.

McDermid (1965), using a sample of fifty-eight male engineers and technical personnel, found that the Revised Art Scale was unrelated to either peer or supervisory ratings of creativity.

To summarize, the Barron-Welsh Art Scale showed positive relationships to creativity in three of five studies. The only study using female subjects found no relationship.

California Psychological Inventory

The California Psychological Inventory (CPI) has been frequently used in criterion-related validation studies. The researchers at the Institute for Personality Assessment Research at Berkeley usually included this test in their assessment battery.

The 480 items of the CPI measure eighteen facets of interpersonal psychology. The subscales are achievement via conformance, achievement via independence, communality, capacity for status, dominance, femininity, flexibility, good impression, intellectual efficiency, psychological-mindedness, responsibility, self-acceptance, self-control, socialization, social presence, sociability, tolerance, and sense of well-being.

Helson and Crutchfield (Helson, 1967, 1971; Helson and Crutchfield, 1970) tested approximately forty-five female and sixty male mathematicians with the CPI. Each mathematician was rated on creativity by other mathematicians. Among the women, creative mathematicians scored significantly higher than a comparison group on flexibility, but lower on communality and achievement via conformance. Among the males, creative mathematicians scored significantly higher than a comparison group on flexibility but lower on self-control. Other subscale scores were nonsignificant.

In a number of places, MacKinnon (1962a, 1962b, 1964, 1965) has reported results on the CPI for 124 male architects. Forty of the architects were rated creative by a variety of knowledgeable persons including professors of architecture. Two control groups of about forty architects each were also used.

The first control group, composed of architects who had worked in the same firms as the creative architects, were very similar to the creative architects on the CPI. On only one scale was there a significant difference between these groups: the creative architects scored lower on the communality scale.

The second control group consisted of 41 architects who had not worked with any of the creative architects. In comparison with the second control group, the creative group scored significantly higher on femininity, flexibility, psychological-mindedness, self-acceptance, and social presence; the creative group scored significantly lower than the second control group on achievement via conformance, communality, good impression, responsibility, socialization, self-control, tolerance, and sense of well-being.

Parloff, Datta, Kleman, and Handlon (1968) factor analyzed CPI scores obtained from the Institute for Personality Assessment Research on four samples: male mathematicians, research scientists, writers, and architects. Several studies (Helson and Crutchfield, 1970; MacKinnon, 1962a, 1962b, 1964, 1965) using these same data have been previously reviewed. Parloff and his colleagues pooled the four samples and obtained four factors from a factor analysis using the Varimax procedure. Creatives and noncreatives were compared on each of the four factors. The results are interesting but of limited use in the current review, since the factors do not precisely correspond to any of the scales of the California Psychological Inventory. Nevertheless, it should be noted that factor 3, which Parloff et al. entitled "adaptive autonomy," showed high loadings from the flexibility and achievement via independence scales. All four creative groups showed higher scores on this factor than the less creative groups.

In summary, the flexibility scale of the CPI appears to be positively related to real-life creativity, while the self-control and the achievement via conformance scales appear to be negatively related to creativity criteria.

Mosaic Construction Test

In the Mosaic Construction Test (Hall, 1972; MacKinnon, 1962b), the subject is given a large selection of one-inch squares in twenty-two different colors. He or she is given thirty minutes to use these squares to construct a pleasing, completely filled-in eight-inch by ten-inch mosaic. The finished mosaics are rated on six dimensions: overall artistic merit; use of color; use of form; originality; warmth or vitality; and pleasingness. The number of colors used is also counted.

Gough (1961) gave Hall's Mosaic Productions Test to forty-five male industrial research scientists. Peer and supervisory ratings were combined to form a single creativity criterion. This criterion was unrelated to five methods of scoring the test. These five methods are not explained further.

Helson (1971), testing twenty-nine female mathematicians, found mosaic designs made by a creative group were judged significantly higher in artistic merit and in pleasingness than those made by a comparison group. Creative and comparison groups were selected on the basis of ratings by other mathematicians.

MacKinnon (1962b), studying forty architects rated highly creative by editors of architectural journals, found a significant correlation between the creativity ratings and ratings of overall artistic merit of the finished mosaics. The mosaics were rated by four university art faculty.

In two of three studies, the overall artistic merit scale has shown positive relationships with creativity. More research is needed to confirm these encouraging results.

Self-Description Inventory (Initiative Scale)

The Self-Description Inventory (Ghiselli, 1954) consists of thirty-two positive and thirty-two negative pairs of adjectives. For the first thirty-two pairs, the subject chooses the adjective that is more descriptive of himself, while, for the second thirty-two pairs, he chooses the adjective that is less descriptive of himself. The initiative scale consists of seventeen of these items which are weighted according to their discriminating power in Ghiselli's (1955) study of college students.

Chambers (1964) administered the initiative scale to 225 male chemists and 213 male psychologists. In both samples he found the creative subjects had significantly higher scores (i.e., more initiative). Creative subjects were chosen on the basis of national recognition and expert peer evaluation.

The Self-Description Inventory appears promising as a measure of scientific creativity.

Sixteen Personality Factor Questionnaire

On this test, sixteen primary factor scales are scored: reserved vs. outgoing (A); less vs. more intelligent (B); affected by feelings vs. emotionally stable (C); humble vs. assertive (E); sober vs. happy-go-lucky (F); expedient vs. conscientious (G); shy vs. venturesome (H); tough-minded vs. tender-minded (I); trusting vs. suspicious (L); practical vs. imaginative (M); forthright vs. shrewd (N); placid vs. apprehensive (O); conservative vs. experimenting (Q1); group-dependent vs. self-sufficient (Q2); undisciplined self-conflict vs. controlled (Q3); and relaxed vs. tense (Q4). A number of second-order factors can also be scored. A higher score on a factor means a subject is closer to the second adjective given to describe the factor.

Chambers (1964) gave scales E, F, H, M, and Q2 from the Sixteen Personality Factor Questionnaire to 225 male chemists and 213 male psychologists. Creative chemists scored significantly higher than control chemists on the E (humble vs. assertive) scale; creative psychologists scored significantly higher than control psychologists on the E and Q2 (group-dependent vs. self-sufficient) scales. Creative subjects were chosen on the basis of national recognition and expert peer evaluation.

Drevdahl (1961, 1964) asked 228 eminent American psychologists (plus 12 additional psychologists) to rate each other for creativity. About 80 percent completed the ratings. On the basis of these ratings, Drevdahl formed four groups: (1) a creative group consisting of 18 highly rated psychologists; (2) a noncreative, nonproductive group consisting of seven psychologists who were rated as having potential for creativity but who had shown no tendency toward creative effort; (3) a noncreative, productive group, consisting of five productive psychologists of average creativity; and (4) a combined control group, consisting of the twelve psychologists in groups 2 and 3.

In the analysis of the Sixteen Personality Factor Questionnaire, Drevdahl compared the creative group separately to each of the other three groups. (It should again be noted that groups 2 and 3 together comprised group 4.) The creative group was significantly higher than the noncreative, nonproductive group in factor H (shy vs. venturesome) and significantly lower on factors M (practical vs. imaginative), O (placid vs. apprehensive), and Q4 (relaxed vs. tense). The creative group was significantly higher than the noncreative productive group on factors G (expedient vs. conscientious) and N (forthright vs. shrewd) and significantly lower on factors E (humble vs. assertive), F (sober vs. happy-go-lucky), and H (shy vs. venturesome). The creative group was significantly higher than the combined control group on factor G (expedient vs. conscientious) and significantly lower on factor F (sober vs. happy-go-lucky).

Drevdahl's findings are of limited importance because he used small groups and overlapping analyses.

Jones (1964) studied eighty-eight male industrial scientists and technologists whose creativity was rated by managerial personnel. Using a unique procedure, Jones found "valid" positive relationships between the creativity ratings and factors C (affected by feelings vs. emotionally stable), E (humble vs. assertive), H (shy vs. venturesome), and Q1 (conservative vs. experimenting). A negative relationship was found with factor O (placid vs. apprehensive).

To summarize, the fairly strong relationship between creativity and factor E indicates that creative scientists are relatively assertive.

Strong Vocational Interest Blank

The Strong Vocational Interest Blank (SVIB) com-pares an individual's interests with those of successful persons in various occupations (Campbell, 1969; Strong, 1966). There are separate versions of the Strong for men and women. The men's version yields eighty-nine scores, including twenty-two basic interest scores, fifty-nine oc-cupational scores, and eight nonoccupational scores. The women's version yields fifty-seven scores, including nine-teen basic interest scores, thirty-four occupational scores, and four nonoccupational scores. These numbers have changed as scales have been added over the years.

Gough (1961) tested forty-five industrial research sci-entists with the SVIB. Only one of fifty-seven scales correlated significantly with a creativity criterion con-sisting of combined peer and supervisory ratings of cre-ativity: the purchasing agent scale correlated negatively with the creativity criterion. This lone finding could reasonably be attributed to chance.

Helson (1971) gave the SVIB to about forty-five female mathematicians who were rated for creativity by other mathematicians. Creativity showed significant positive relationships with the artist, psychologist, physicist, and author-journalist scales, and a significant negative re-lationship with the mortician scale.

Helson and Crutchfield (1970) tested twenty-seven/thirty-four creative and twenty-nine comparison male mathematicians with the SVIB. Creativity was rated by experts in mathematics. Creatives scored significantly lower than comparison men on vocational agricultural teacher, aviator, mathematics-science teacher, police-man, and forest service man. The creative subjects had significantly higher scores on president of manufactur-ing concern.

MacKinnon (MacKinnon, 1964; Hall and MacKinnon, 1969), studying 124 male architects rated for creativity by experts in architecture, reported that forty of fifty-seven regular and special scales of the SVIB were significantly related to creativity. The five scales positively correlated most highly were: artist (.59), author-journalist (.54), lawyer (.44), advertising man (.42), and musician (.38); the five scales most negatively correlated were: banker (−.66), office man (−.60), accountant (−.54), policeman (−.52), and purchasing agent (−.50).

The following is a listing of all scales that showed significant correlations with the architects' creativity ratings:

Positive Relationships
artist
psychologist
architect
physician
osteopath
dentist
physicist
chemist
city school superintendent
minister
musician
sales manager
advertising man
lawyer
author-journalist
president of manufacturing concern
clinical psychologist
V.A. clinical psychologist
psychiatrist
specialization level

Negative Relationships
production manager
mathematics and physical science teacher
printer
industrial arts teacher
farmer
aviator
carpenter
vocational agricultural teacher
forest service man
policeman
senior C.P.A.
purchasing agent
accountant
office man
banker
real estate salesman
guidance psychologist
industrial psychologist
army officer
masculinity-femininity

Moffie and Goodner (1968) obtained supervisory ratings and rankings of creativity, a self-ranking of creativity, and a combined creativity product index (e.g., patents) for seventy-six males educated as chemical engineers. Most held management positions at the time of the ratings. These criteria were correlated with SVIB scores obtained fifteen to twenty years earlier, when the subjects were in college. The SVIB was scored for six basic interests (biological sciences; engineering and physical sciences; social service and welfare occupations; business detail and administration; sales or business contact; and verbal or linguistic occupations), for four occupational scales (engineer, chemist, production manager, and personnel manager), and for occupational level. The only correlation that reached significance was between the occupational level scores and supervisory ratings of creativity.

Donald Taylor (1963) administered the SVIB to 103 male electronics engineers and electronics scientists. Only the engineering scale of the test was scored, and Taylor found no significant correlation between this scale and ratings of creativity by supervisors.

The Strong Vocational Interest Blank may be helpful in identifying creative scientists. Positive relationships with creativity have been found for the artist, psychologist, physicist, author-journalist, and president-of-manufacturing-concern scales. Negative relationships have been found for vocational-agricultural-teacher, aviator, mathematics-science-teacher, policeman, and forest-service-man scales. The remaining scales have not shown consistent relationships.

PERSONAL HISTORY QUESTIONNAIRES

A number of instruments of the personal history questionnaire type have been constructed during the last twenty years. The personal history questionnaires typically include items not only about past experiences but also about present interests, activities, and attitudes. Since personal history questionnaires generally show relationships to creativity criteria in science, all studies using these measures are summarized in this chapter rather than in an appendix. The following measures are reviewed on subsequent pages:

Biographical Inventory
Biographical Information for Research and Scientific Talent
Buel's Biographical Personal History Form
Chambers' Biographical Inventory
CREE Questionnaire
Life History Questionnaire
Smith, Albright, Glennon, and Owens' Personal History Questionnaire
Donald Taylor's Biographical Questionnaire
Ypma's Biographical Questionnaire

Biographical Inventory

Two studies using the biographical approach (Ellison, 1960; Taylor, Smith, Ghiselin, and Ellison, 1961) laid the groundwork for the Biographical Inventory. Cross-validation designs were not used, but both studies were useful in selecting items for subsequent research.

Taylor and his co-workers (Taylor and Ellison, 1964, 1967; Taylor, Ellison, and Tucker, 1965) reported four cross-validation studies using various forms of the Biographical Inventory with NASA scientists. In the first study, 354 male NASA scientists were given Form A, consisting of 300 items, of the Biographical Inventory. Three creativity criteria were used: (1) a creativity checklist;[3] (2) a creativity rating scale; and (3) the sum of publications and patents. The first two criteria were obtained from supervisors. The sample was split, and the cross-validity of the best biographical score, when related to a combination of the first two creativity criteria, was .59.

---

3. The creativity checklist, of which there are several forms, consisits of a series of statements that an evaluator checks if sthey describe the person being rated (see D. W. Taylor, 1958). Each statement has a creativity scale value, which was empirically determined. A person's rating is the median value of the statements checked.

In the second validation study, 300 NASA scientists were given a modified form of the Biographical Inventory (Form B), also with 300 items. The criterion was a creativity rating scale completed by supervisors. Using scoring keys developed in the first study, Taylor and Ellison found the average cross-validity coefficient for a total creativity biographical score was .47 against the creativity rating scale.

In a third study, 769 NASA scientists were given another form of the Biographical Inventory (Form C). Supervisors' creativity ratings were the criterion relevant to this review. The scoring keys developed in the first study were again related to the creativity criterion, and an average cross-validity of .40 was obtained.

A fourth study (Taylor, Ellison, and Tucker, 1965) involved a predictive design rather than the concurrent design that had been used in the three studies reported above. Form C-1 of the Biographical Inventory was given to 622 NASA scientists. Form C-1 is identical to Form C except that the instructions are slightly modified. Supervisors completed creativity of work ratings and a creativity checklist for each person. Cross-validities on the total sample ranged from .15 to .20, using three keys developed in prior studies. Additional analyses were also presented using subsamples of the 622 scientists. The cross-validities with the subsamples were also generally low. Irregularities in data collection, as well as the use of a predictive rather than concurrent design, may account for the disappointing results in this study.

Ellison, James, and Carron (1970) administered a 200-item form of the Biographical Inventory to 203 scientists and engineers. Among the criteria used were a creativity rating and a creativity checklist, both completed by a subject's immediate supervisor. The sample was divided into two groups for cross-validation purposes. Cross-validities were .40 and .47 for the creativity rating, and .26 and .41 for the creativity checklist.

A 160-item biographical inventory was related to a

composite creativity criterion (based on supervisory, self, and subordinate ratings) for 157 male pharmaceutical scientists (Cline, Tucker, and Anderson, 1966). Most of the items used were taken from Taylor and Ellison's Biographical Inventory. A creativity key developed at NASA by Calvin Taylor and his associates correlated .35 with the creativity criterion.

Tucker, Cline, and Schmitt (1967) reanalyzed the data from the Cline, Tucker, and Anderson (1966) study. But this time, the sample of 157 was split into two samples of 78 and 79 subjects. For each sample, a creativity key was constructed to relate to a new composite creativity criterion, this one consisting of combined supervisory, peer, and subordinate ratings of creativity. Each of the two creativity keys thus constructed was then cross-validated on the other sample. The cross-validities for the two creativity keys were .36 and .42.

Moffie and Goodner (1968) administered a 160-item version of Taylor and Ellison's Biographical Inventory to seventy-six males who were originally educated as chemical engineers but most of whom were occupying management positions. Each person had to ask his immediate supervisor to complete a rating form which included a creativity rating. The overall creativity score from the Biographical Inventory was significantly correlated both with this creativity rating and with a combined creativity product index (e.g., patents).

On the basis of these studies, we can conclude that the various forms of the Biographical Inventory show consistent relationships with scientific creativity.

Biographical Information for
Research and Scientific Talent

McDermid (1965) administered the ninety-six-item Biographical Information for Research and Scientific Talent (BIRST) form to fifty-eight male engineers and technicians. The creativity rating key of the BIRST was significantly correlated with both peer and supervisory ratings of creativity.

Buel's Biographical Personal History Form

Buel (1965) used many items from two earlier studies by Albright and his colleagues (Albright and Glennon, 1961; Smith, Albright, Glennon, and Owens, 1961). Buel's 118-item biographical personal history form was given to 132 male pharmaceutical researchers. Subjects were rated for potential to make "significant, original, and lasting contributions to research" by two evaluators. A supervisor's evaluation of creativity was also obtained. Buel divided his total sample into an item-weighting sample of eighty and a cross-validating sample of fifty-two. Two keys were constructed. Cross-validity coefficients of about .50 were found for the first criterion for both keys. For the second criterion, the supervisor's evaluation of creativity, there were low cross-validities for both keys.

Chambers' Biographical Inventory

Chambers (1964) administered an eighty-one-item biographical inventory of his own construction to 213 male psychologists and 225 male chemists. Twenty items significantly differentiated between creative and comparison psychologists; twenty-six did so between creative and comparison chemists. Creative subjects were chosen on the basis of national recognition and expert peer evaluation.

CREE Questionnaire

Louis and Thelma Thurstone and John Mellinger developed this test in the late 1950s (Burns, Harris, and Hendrix, 1957; Thurstone and Mellinger, 1959). Although not strictly speaking a personal history questionnaire, the types of items used are similar to those employed in such questionnaires.

The 145 items in the CREE Questionnaire were chosen from a pool of 377 items by comparing 142 engineers who were successful, creative inventors with 141 engineers who were not (Thurstone and Mellinger, 1959). All subjects were identified by chief engineers. Use of the 89 most significant items correctly identified 78 percent of the 283 engineers. No cross-validation was reported.

Life History Questionnaire

The 181-item Life History Questionnaire was used by Owens (1969) in a study of 457 research and development engineers. The Life History Questionnaire deals primarily with a subject's demographic characteristics and experiential background, but ten criterion items are also included, such as the number of papers presented at professional meetings and the number of patents held. These ten criterion items were removed and weighted to form a criterion score for each subject. The criterion score seems to reflect both productivity and creativity. The remaining items from the Life History Questionnaire were factor analyzed, and three personal history factors were found: socioeconomic background, favorable self-perception, and academic achievement. Owens found that both favorable self-perception and academic achievement showed small but significant negative relationships with the criterion.

Smith, Albright, Glennon, and
Owens' Personal History Questionnaire

Smith, Albright, Glennon, and Owens (1961) administered a 484-item personal history questionnaire to between 198 and 331 research scientists. The number varied because of missing predictor or criterion data. A checklist rating scale for creativity was one of the criteria. However, since some of the same individuals were used both in the construction of the keys and in the cross-validation of the keys, the results of this study cannot be relied upon.

Donald Taylor's Biographical Questionnaire

Donald Taylor (1963) administered a 50-item biographical questionnaire to ninety-four male electronics engineers and electronics scientists and to sixty-six male physicists. Different creativity criteria were used with the two samples. For the electronics personnel, seven of the items were significantly related to supervisors' ratings of creativity. However, for the physicists, none of the items was significantly related to supervisors' ratings of originality.

Ypma's Biographical Questionnaire

Ypma (1968) gave a 143-item biographical questionnaire to 395 scientists. These scientists included 320 chemists and chemical engineers. Of the total sample, 93 percent were male, and 31 percent held Ph.D.'s. Items were selected from those used in previous research (e.g., Chambers, 1964; Smith, Albright, Glennon, and Owens, 1961). Ypma combined supervisors' ratings on a creativity checklist (D. Taylor, 1963) with a composite creativity score based on products (e.g., patents, publications) to form a total creativity criterion.

An a priori, non-empirical key correlated .42 with the product-based composite creativity score and .40 with the supervisors' ratings of creativity.

An empirical key produced cross-validities of .35 and .55 for the total creativity criterion when the chemists and chemical engineers were split into two groups of 160 each. When applied to the seventy-five scientists from other disciplines, this key yielded cross-validities of .42 for the composite criterion, .65 for the supervisors' ratings, and .63 for the total creativity criterion.

Personal History Questionnaires:
Further Notes

These questionnaires have been quite successful in relating to creative accomplishments in science. Studies consistently yield cross-validity coefficients of about .40.

The range of items that have been used in personal history questionnaires is very broad. Typical of the items that have been found to be related to scientific creativity are the following from Ypma (1968):

A. Regarding responsibility in your job, would you
  + 1. Like to have a good deal of responsibility?
  − 2. Like to have some responsibility, but still have someone responsible over you?
    3. Prefer a minimum of responsibility?
    4. Rather not have any responsibility?

+ means response is positively correlated with creativity criteria.
− means response is negatively correlated with creativity criteria.

B. Did you ever build an apparatus or device of your own design on *your own initiative* and not as part of any *required* school assignment during your later school years?
    1. Yes—in high school
  + 2. Yes—in college
  + 3. Yes—both in high school and college
  − 4. No

C. On the average, I keep up with the articles in:
  − 1. No scientific journals
  − 2. One or two scientific journals
    3. Three or four scientific journals
    4. Five or six scientific journals
  + 5. More than six scientific journals

D. During college I was a member of:
  + 1. More than two honor societies
    2. Two honor societies
    3. One honor society
  − 4. No honor societies

DISCUSSION

Of the three types of measures reviewed here, the personal history questionnaires showed the most consistent relationships with creative accomplishments in science. Less consistent relationships were found for the personality, vocational, and miscellaneous tests. The cognitive tests were least often related to scientific creativity. We will discuss our findings separately for the three classes of tests.

Personal History Questionnaires

The results from studies using the personal history inventories indicate that certain life experiences may facilitate later creativity. Which kinds of life experiences relate to later creativity is a question which cannot be fully answered here, because the creativity scoring keys for some of the personal history inventories are not publicly available. But when available, the findings from such questionnaires can be used to identify personal experiences and characteristics related to creative accomplishment. These findings will be discussed later, especially in chapters 3, 4, and 6.

Personality, Vocational, and Miscellaneous Tests

The findings for these tests were encouraging. Seven tests showed some fairly consistent relationships with scientific creativity. In chapter 3, we develop the implications of these findings for a theory of the characteristics of auctorive persons. We believe that there are a few personality traits predisposing people toward creativity generally and several other traits associated with creativity in specialized areas.

Cognitive and Perceptual Tests

In general, the cognitive and perceptual tests showed few relationships to scientific creativity. None of the perceptual tests (Gestalt Transformation Test, Gestalt Completion Test, Gottschaldt Figures Test) showed any relationships to scientific creativity.

Of the cognitive tests, the divergent thinking tests are of special interest because of their widespread use. Commonly used measures such as the Unusual Uses tests and the Consequences tests have shown almost no evidence of criterion-related validity with scientists.

Defenders of divergent thinking tests can, of course, point to several possible reasons for the failure of these tests to relate to real-life scientific creativity. First, since the scientists used in most of the studies were substantially above average in IQ (and no doubt in other abilities), and since some divergent thinking abilities have been shown to be positively correlated with IQ (Wallach, 1968), the predictive power of divergent thinking tests may have been somewhat limited.[4] Second, some scientists may have regarded the tests as trivial or childish, so that test performance was not a valid indicator of ability. Unless there is moderate motivation to persist in generating ideas, high scores may reflect willingness to follow instructions as much as superior divergent thinking ability. Third, there are the reasons mentioned by Guilford (1971): inappropriate or unreliable creativity criteria and low reliability of some divergent thinking tests.

The findings of a study by Myron S. Allen, reported in detail by J. P. Guilford (1963), suggest that divergent thinking abilities are generally overemphasized for scientists. Two groups of subjects ranked twenty-eight aptitude factors for their importance to the creative scientist. One group was composed of persons engaged in scientific or engineering research; a second group was

---

4. Selecting a sample (e.g., scientists) with a restricted range on one of the variables under consideration (e.g., divergent thinking ability) typically yields a correlation that underestimates the size of the correlation that exists in the general population (e.g., American adults).

composed of nonresearchers attending the annual Creative Problem Solving Institute at the University of Buffalo in 1958. By far, the greatest discrepancy in rankings between the two groups occurred for the divergent thinking factors of spontaneous flexibility and ideational fluency. The Institute participants ranked these factors 3 and 6, respectively, while the researchers in science and engineering ranked them 14.5 and 19, respectively. Since these two divergent thinking abilities are among the major factors in most widely used creativity tests (e.g., Torrance Tests of Creative Thinking, Wallach-Kogan tests), this study suggests that persons actively engaged in scientific research do not agree with the conventional wisdom in creativity circles concerning the importance of divergent thinking.

Of course, the findings of the Allen study cannot readily be generalized to persons in nonscientific fields; such persons may well subscribe to the importance of divergent thinking abilities in their work. Some evidence bearing indirectly on this point is provided by Hudson (1966), who administered both divergent and convergent tests to British schoolboys. Hudson found that arts specialists scored higher on divergent than convergent tests, whereas science specialists showed the reverse pattern.

It is possible that additional research will provide evidence for the criterion-related validity of divergent thinking tests for auctors in nonscientific fields; but virtually no such research has been published. In addition, divergent thinking tests may be useful as measures of creativity below the auctorive level. For example, several studies (Bartlett and Davis, 1974; Kogan and Pankove, 1972, 1974; Wallach and Wing, 1969) show some positive relationships between the Wallach and Kogan tests (1965) and a variety of nonacademic attainments in elementary, high school, and college students.

3

Creative
Scientists

IN THIS CHAPTER, WE FOCUS on the personal characteristics of creative scientists. We shall first try to
identify those characteristics which have shown some
consistency in differentiating creative from less creative
scientists. Later, we shall speculate about the role of
personal characteristics in the development of auctorive
scientific creativity.

Before identifying the personal characteristics, however, we would like to comment on the ways in which
our approach differs from that of the many other psychologists (e.g., Chambers, 1969; Dellas and Gaier, 1970;
Torrance, 1962) who have written about personal characteristics associated with creativity. First, other writers
have included many characteristics which have received
little or no support in studies of auctors. Divergent
thinking abilities, considered by many writers (e.g.,
Chambers, 1969; Guilford, 1967a) to be important to
creativity, are a case in point. Accordingly, we shall

focus on the few auctorive characteristics which have received empirical support in studies using real-life creativity criteria.

Second, some writers have not always relied on evidence from persons showing real-life creative performance. Some writers have searched for personal characteristics associated with creativity test performance. But since no creativity test has consistently shown high correlations with measures of real-life creativity, we believe that the only way to understand real-life creativity is to study it directly.

A third way in which our approach differs from that of other psychologists is that we limit our focus to science and related fields. Other psychologists have often assumed that personal characteristics of creative persons hold across fields as diverse as art, writing, and science. Although this position may be correct, there is little evidence for it. Almost all the studies relating real-life creativity to personal characteristics have been conducted with persons in scientific and related fields. Accordingly, we shall not attempt to generalize beyond scientifically oriented fields.

We believe there is a continuum of creativity among auctors. Publishing original research is not the same as doing Nobel prize-winning work. We tentatively assume, however, that the personal characteristics associated with creativity at the lower end of the auctorive continuum are also associated with creativity at the higher end of the continuum.

In the studies of auctors, a special problem is posed by the abundance of inconsistent results. To be sure, several characteristics have shown fair consistency in differentiating auctors from less creative persons. Still, it is common to find a characteristic differentiating auctors in one study but not in others. Inconsistent results are to be expected when studies sample subjects from different fields, use different criteria for identifying creative and less creative subgroups, and employ research designs differing in the sophistication of methodological controls. We list only those characteristics which have shown consistency across fields. The evidence supporting these characteristics is briefly discussed.

CHARACTERISTICS NECESSARY FOR A SCIENTIFIC CAREER

The first three characteristics to be considered should be viewed as preconditions for the attainment of a professional level of expertise in a field. These preconditions differentiate auctors from the general public, although not from less creative professionals in the same field.

Above Average Intelligence

Most researchers studying auctors have reported that auctors possess substantially above average intelligence (e.g., Barron, 1969; Helson, 1971; MacKinnon, 1962a; Roe, 1965). A high IQ is probably necessary for admission to and completion of an advanced graduate program. However, as is apparent from the criterion-related validity studies of intelligence tests, which are reviewed in Appendix A, a high IQ does not usually differentiate creative from less creative professionals in the same field. A threshold effect seems to operate for IQ (MacKinnon, 1968b; Meer and Stein, 1955), such that, above a certain level required for mastery of a field, IQ is not correlated with creativity. The IQ threshold probably varies from one field to another; it is probably higher in scientific than in artistic fields.

More specific mental abilities, which are required for auctorive creativity in particular fields, probably show similar threshold effects. Examples of such abilities include numerical ability in mathematics, spatial ability in architecture, and verbal ability in prose or poetry. Other mental abilities may be important in music and art.

Extensive Training in a Field

This characteristic is a self-evident condition for creative accomplishment in most areas of human endeavor (e.g., Ypma, 1968). Most fields are sufficiently differentiated that aspiring auctors must master the existing knowledge and theory in an area before they have a chance of making a creative contribution. This mastery is normally attained in graduate degree programs, which demand for their completion a high degree of persistence.

Emotional Adjustment

A minimal level of emotional adjustment is another self-evident requirement for auctorive creativity. The level of adjustment must be high enough to allow sustained work to be done (Roe, 1951b). Thus a low threshold probably operates for this characteristic. Although there is abundant anecdotal evidence about auctors' adjustment or lack thereof, little systematic research has been conducted on this topic. One relevant finding is Chambers' (1964) report that both creative and comparison groups of chemists and psychologists fell in the average range in their feelings of security versus insecurity.

CHARACTERISTICS OF CREATIVE SCIENTISTS

Let us turn from characteristics that are prerequisites for a professional career and consider the personal characteristics distinguishing auctors from less creative persons in the same field.

Autonomy

The independence of auctors is stressed by virtually everyone who has theorized about highly creative adult professionals (e.g., Chambers, 1969; Dellas and Gaier, 1970). This independence and rejection of outside influences has been documented for architects (MacKinnon, 1962a, 1962b, 1964), petroleum research scientists (Morrison, 1961), research chemists (Stein, 1962, 1963; Ypma, 1968), physical and biological scientists (Roe, 1951a, 1951b, 1952, 1953), industrial research scientists (Ypma, 1968), and female mathematicians (Helson, 1971). For example, MacKinnon (1962a), describing his creative architects, viewed independence as a central trait, already well-established when the architects were in college:

> They were unwilling to accept anything on the mere say-so of their instructors. Nothing was to be accepted on faith or because it had behind it the voice of authority. Such matters might be accepted, but only after the student on his own had demonstrated their validity to himself. (P. 494)

Evidence for the independence of auctors also comes from studies, reviewed in chapter 2, showing these persons consistently score higher than less creative professionals on the autonomy scale of the Adjective Check List.

Personal Flexibility and Openness to Experience

These and similar characteristics have been emphasized by Chambers (1969) and MacKinnon (1962a). The importance of flexibility is supported by research with the flexibility scale of the California Psychological Inventory, which has differentiated auctors from less creative persons in a variety of fields (see chapter 2). The items on this scale appear to tap tolerance for uncertainty and complexity; high scorers are unconcerned with order or strict adherence to rules and routines. Additional evidence for the importance of flexibility is provided by Ypma's (1968) finding that industrial research scientists who were more creative preferred a job in which they were "free to experiment with and try new methods."

The importance of openness to experience is supported by studies using the lability scale of the Adjective Check

List (see chapter 2). The lability scale, which has differentiated auctors from less creative adult professionals, appears to identify persons who are open to their emotions and are adventurous and imaginative.

Need to Be Original and Novel

Many researchers (Arieti, 1976; Bergum, 1975; Chambers, 1964; MacKinnon, 1963; Ypma, 1968) have observed that highly creative persons view themselves as creative and consciously strive to be original. Consider, for example, MacKinnon's (1963) description of the creative architects he studied:

> Above all else he [the creative architect] thinks of himself as imaginative; unquestionably committed to creative endeavor; unceasingly striving for creative solutions to the difficult problems he repeatedly sets for himself; satisfied only with solutions which are original and meet his own high standards of architectural excellence. . . . (P. 276)

The more creative scientists studied by Chambers (1964) also expressed a need to be imaginative and original. Chambers found that:

> When seeking a position, the less creative scientists are predominantly concerned with opportunities to combine teaching and administrative duties with research, while the overwhelming choice for the creative scientists is the opportunity to do really creative research and to choose problems of interest to them. (P. 6)

Additional evidence is provided by Ypma (1968), who found that responses to the question, How creative do you feel you are?, validly predicted creativity for three samples of industrial research scientists. When asked about the major motivating force in their lives, the more creative scientists were likely to answer: To come up with something new. First-person accounts of scientists (e.g., Austin, 1978) also give support to the existence of a strong need for originality and novelty in creative scientists.

Other theorists in the creativity area have hypothesized that needs for novelty and originality may be related to creativity. For example, Barron (1963) proposed that creative adults have a disposition toward originality. Similarly, Maddi (1965) suggested that creativity could be partially explained by a need for novelty.[1]

If creative scientists have a need to be original and novel, one might expect them to score higher than less creative scientists on divergent thinking tests. Divergent thinking tests do provide opportunities to be original and novel. Yet the studies reviewed in chapter 2 and appendix A revealed few associations between scientific creativity and performance on such tests. Perhaps scientists' need to be original and novel is expressed only in scientific work and related tasks. Scientists may be unwilling to work creatively on tasks like divergent thinking tests, which they may perceive to be trivial or childish. As Allen (Guilford, 1963) has shown, most scientists do not believe that divergent thinking is central to scientific creativity.

Need for Professional Recognition

This need for recognition by one's peers is often denied by creative persons, yet there is ample evidence for its importance (e.g., Roe, 1965; Merton, 1973). For example, a large number of disputes among scientists have stemmed from priority claims (Merton, 1973, chapters 14 and 18). The existence of honorary societies, honorary degrees, and distinguished achievement awards also testifies to this need.

Creative persons tend to score lower on the deference scale of the Adjective Check List and higher in assertiveness (vs. humbleness) on the Sixteen Personality Factor Questionnaire (see chapter 2). In addition, MacKinnon (1964) reported that an IPAR self-assertive-

---

1. More recently, Maddi (1975) has changed his position on novelty as a motivator for creative endeavor and has suggested instead that creativity may be better explained by the need to avoid alienation.

ness scale was related to creativity in 124 architects. Also, creative male mathematicians placed more emphasis on making their mark in the field than did comparison mathematicians (Helson and Crutchfield, 1970).

Commitment to Work

Studies of auctors consistently show that they work harder and longer and are more productive than their less creative peers (Chambers, 1964; Roe, 1951a, 1951b, 1965; Ypma, 1968). Accounts by creative scientists (e.g., Loewi, 1953) also emphasize this commitment to work. Chambers found that the creative chemists and psychologists he studied read more professional journals, presented more papers at conventions, and produced many more articles than did control groups of chemists and psychologists; this evidence of greater productive energy was also evident while the subjects were still in graduate school.

Often, this work commitment involves the subordination of nearly everything else (Helson, 1971; Roe, 1951b; Ypma, 1968). Roe, for example, described a group of eminent physical scientists as follows:

> There is only one thing which seems to characterize the total group, and that is absorption in their work, over long years, and frequently to the exclusion of everything else. This was also true of the biologists. This one thing alone is probably not of itself sufficient to account for the success enjoyed by these men, but it appears to be a *sine qua non*. It needs to be accompanied by a certain amount of intelligence, and by sufficient emotional and social adjustment that it is possible to maintain a position in which the work can be done. (Pp. 233–34)

The high level of task commitment is coupled with self-directed motivation (Chambers, 1964; MacKinnon, 1961; Ypma, 1968). MacKinnon (1961) observed that his creative architects were strongly motivated to achieve in situations requiring independent thought and action, rather than conformity. Similarly, Chambers (1964), studying creative chemists and psychologists, concluded that the creative scientist

> is not the type of person who waits for someone else to tell him what to do, but rather thinks things through and then takes action on his own with little regard to convention or current "fashion." (P. 14)

The three motivational characteristics we have identified—need to be original and novel, need for professional recognition, and commitment to work—have far-reaching implications for the personal lives of auctors. For example, aspiring auctors, at least at the start of their careers, may find that their need to be original necessitates financial sacrifices. But potentially more serious are the consequences of commitment to work. If the commitment is extreme, family and personal relationships are sure to suffer, and there will be little time for hobbies or activities leading to personal growth. These problems, of course, are not limited to auctors but are the price paid by anyone for whom work is the highest priority.

Aesthetic Sensitivity

Although this characteristic is not well established, there is some evidence that auctors show greater aesthetic sensitivity than their less creative peers. Auctors tend to score high on the Barron-Welsh Art Scale, which taps preference for complex and asymmetrical line drawings; on the Mosaic Construction Test, auctors tend to achieve high ratings of overall artistic merit (see chapter 2). Further evidence for the importance of aesthetic sensensitivity is provided by Clifford's (1958) finding that twelve of seventeen highly creative chemists and mathematicians experienced aesthetic satisfaction from their work. In a similar vein, MacKinnon (1962a) noted that a creative person demands that "solutions be elegant. He seeks both truth and beauty" (p. 490). Also, Zuckerman (1977, p. 128) reported that many Nobel laureates she interviewed "identified 'simplicity' of solutions as a mark of scientific taste." And psychologist L. L. Thurstone (1964, p. 15) expressed the view that "creative scientific work is largely artistic in character." The role of beauty and simplicity in creative scientific work has also been emphasized by Chandrasekhar (1975), an astronomer, Rollo May (1975), a psychoanalyst, and S. M. Ulam (1976), a mathematician.

Summary of Personal Characteristics

A number of characteristics seem applicable to auctors across fields. Above average IQ, extensive training in a field, and at least a minimal level of emotional adjustment function as preconditions necessary for the attainment of a professional level of expertise. Among persons who reach this level, several other characteristics are associated with auctorive creativity and probably contribute to its development. These include the need to be original and novel, the need for professional recognition, commitment to work, personal flexibility, openness to experience, and autonomy. Aesthetic sensitivity may be an additional characteristic, although the evidence for its importance is less well established.

A MODEL OF AUCTORIVE CREATIVITY

Virtually all scientists seem to have certain characteristics necessary for a scientific career: high intelligence, extensive training, and at least moderate socioemotional adjustment. But the more creative scientists are also likely to show high levels on the six other characteristics we enumerated: autonomy, personal flexibility, need to be original and novel, need for professional recognition, commitment to work, and aesthetic sensitivity. On the basis of these findings, we offer a model which, though frankly speculative, can explain a number of phenomena associated with auctorive creativity. We believe that the six personal characteristics of the more creative scientists all operate as causal influences, each increasing the likelihood that a scientist will produce creative work. We concede that the six characteristics, since they do appear with *adult* scientists, could logically be viewed as outcomes rather than causes of scientific creativity. To some extent, the relationships are probably bi-directional; but the evidence clearly suggests that these personal characteristics are more causes than effects. For example, there is evidence (Chambers, 1964; MacKinnon, 1962a; Ypma, 1968) that the characteristics of auctors were already well established when the auctors were in graduate school, long before they received professional recognition.

If a person is to become a creative scientist, he must first show the prerequisites of high intelligence, extensive training, and moderate socio-emotional adjustment. In addition, he must be generally high on the personal characteristics: low levels on one or two personal characteristics might occur, but they could be compensated for by unusually high levels on other personal characteristics. There is also the likelihood that the combination of disposing characteristics is multiplicative rather than additive (Meehl, 1965); and curvilinear relationships are possible, as well. The personal characteristics thus operate as predictor variables in a multiple regression equation which has creativity as the criterion variable.

Our model suggests reasons why the personal characteristics, when considered separately, show relatively small correlations with scientific creativity. If creativity depends on the joint occurrence of high levels on several characteristics, many scientists showing high levels on one of the characteristics will nevertheless show little evidence of creativity, because other important characteristics may be absent or present only at low levels. Allison and Stewart (1974, p. 597) have hypothesized that, as tasks become less routine, more characteristics of the individual become relevant to performance, with the result that the distribution of task performance becomes increasingly skewed. Although many persons have one or several of the relevant characteristics, only a few persons have all the characteristics necessary for task performance. Since creative science is anything but routine, it should require a number of different individual characteristics, most of which can be expected to show only small correlations with scientific creativity.

This view of auctorive creativity contradicts the conception of creativity as a normally distributed trait (e.g., Blade, 1963). This conception is not merely a straw man. As Ausubel (1968) and Nicholls (1972) pointed out, much creativity research with children and adolescents has implicitly or explicitly assumed creativity is a normally distributed trait.

The personal characteristics should be viewed as relatively stable adult traits. They are neither immutable nor easily changed. They evolve gradually and become crystallized into fairly permanent traits once the scientists have become entrenched in their careers. Rewards, punishments, models, and situational factors (e.g., university or industrial work settings) probably influence the personal characteristics to some degree.

How do the personal characteristics lead to creative scientific accomplishments? To some extent, this question has already been answered. The personal characteristics influence the scientist's choice of job and choice of research problems. It seems self-evident that these choices then affect the chances of creative accomplishments. More directly, the personal characteristics influence the quantity and quality of work.

One advantage of the model is that it can explain the rareness of auctorive creativity. Many talented persons do not become auctors because they are very low on one or several of the personal characteristics. As a result, there are relatively few scientists who manifest high creativity but many who manifest little or none. A skewed distribution of creativity is consistent with the log normal distribution of number of publications by scientific personnel found by Shockley (1957).

Our model suggests the existence of different types of auctors. Detailed speculation would be premature, but types might be identified on the basis of unusually high levels on one or a few of the personal characteristics. For example, one type of auctor with an exceptionally high commitment to work might achieve creativity primarily through methodical plodding and dogged perseverance. Another type, high on flexibility and openness to experience, might achieve innovative insights by viewing a problem in terms of an analogy drawn from some field outside the field of the problem. Many different types of auctors can be derived from the proposed model, with ample room for individual eccentricity.

One important limitation of the model deserves mention: creativity is predicted only from a set of personal characteristics. But since auctorive creativity must occur at a particular time and in a particular social milieu, situational and societal factors may also facilitate or impede its expression. In Robert Merton's view (1973, p. 366), all discoveries would eventually be made independently by several persons because the appropriate environmental determinants are present. But Merton believes that "scientists of genius" can speed up this process because they can do the work of many average scientists.

As psychologists, we believe situational and societal factors may influence the personal characteristics that facilitate creativity. Merton, as a sociologist, takes the view that personal characteristics may facilitate or impede the workings of situational and societal forces.

The Role of Chance in Scientific Creativity

A model predicting scientific creativity on the basis of personal characteristics of scientists may appear overly deterministic, and some critics will argue we have neglected the role of chance in creativity. It cannot be denied that factors of chance often influence creative discoveries. For this reason, any model based on a set of personal characteristics will always predict creativity imperfectly. However, chance often does not operate in isolation to affect creativity; in many cases, it works in conjunction with scientists' personal characteristics.

This point is perhaps best supported in Austin's book (1978) on the role of chance in scientific creativity. Austin identifies four types of chance. Chance I, or blind luck, does not depend on any personal characteristics of the recipient. But three other types of chance are directly linked to personal characteristics. In Chance II, good luck results from general exploratory behavior. That is, a scientist's energetic scientific activity increases the likelihood that random ideas in fresh combinations will lead to creative discoveries. According to Austin, Chance II depends on "curiosity about many things, persistence, willingness to experiment and to explore" (p. 78). These characteristics are closely related to ones we have discussed in our own model. Curiosity about many things seems related to the need to be original and novel; persistence is related to commitment to work; willingness to experiment and to explore is related to personal flexibility and openness to experience.

Austin's Chance III exemplifies Louis Pasteur's statement that chance favors the prepared mind. In Chance III, chance occurs in the form of a faint clue which is overlooked by everyone except a scientist who, because of training and experience, is uniquely prepared to observe it and to grasp its significance. Austin believes Chance III depends on the scientist's background of knowledge and on abilities to observe, remember, and quickly form significant new associations. In terms of our own model, above average intelligence, extensive training in a field, commitment to work, and personal flexibility all seem related to Chance III.

Austin's Chance IV expresses the principle that chance favors the individualized action. Fortuitous events occur when the scientist acts in a highly personalized way. Distinctive hobbies, personal lifestyles, and activities peculiar to the scientist as an individual may lead to a discovery. In terms of our own model, autonomy and generalized personal flexibility would increase the likelihood a scientist would have an unusual hobby or a distinctive lifestyle which could act as a catalyst for Chance IV.

In many cases, then, chance operates in conjunction with the personal characteristics we have found in creative scientists. We will return to the role of chance in chapter 5.

THE CULTIVATION OF SCIENTIFIC CREATIVITY

Our model suggests no simple guidelines for fostering scientific creativity. One must begin by selecting highly intelligent persons and educating them in science. Those who would enhance creativity might also consider influencing the development of relevant personal characteristics.

Each of these personal characteristics can probably be influenced by a variety of experiences at different times of life. Flexibility, for example, is probably influenced by parent-child interaction beginning in early childhood, by the breadth of experiences encountered over a lifetime, and by adult models encountered in and out of school, especially during adolescence. Since the profiles of creative scientists vary considerably on personal characteristics, many different antecedents of auctorive creativity must be possible. This diversity might explain why so few family and child-rearing variables have shown relationships to creativity. We shall review the evidence linking creativity to family and child-rearing variables in chapter 4.

Some experiences crucial to the development of scientific creativity may not occur until adulthood. One such experience may be an apprenticeship with a master in the field (Wallach, 1976). The apprenticeship seems especially important at the highest levels of scientific creativity. For example, Zuckerman (1965, 1977) reported that more than half of American Nobel prize winners worked, as young scientists, under Nobel prize winners of earlier generations. Chambers (1973) also found that the development of creative scientists was strongly influenced by long-term, one-to-one experiences with professors in graduate school.

Can scientific creativity be attained through training? Training for creativity has been a perennial concern of some creativity researchers and many educators. Existing creativity training programs (e.g., Feldhusen, Treffinger, and Bahlke, 1970; Parnes, Noller, and Biondi, 1977) often attempt to influence divergent thinking abilities. But there is little evidence that these abilities are important to scientific creativity. Studies of these programs, therefore, can tell us little about the possibility of training for scientific creativity (e.g., Mansfield and Busse, 1974; Mansfield, Busse, and Krepelka, 1978). However, programs like the ones developed at Johns Hopkins University for gifted and talented youth are effective in helping youngsters master subjects such as mathematics at a greatly increased rate (Keating, 1976; Stanley, George, and Solano, 1977; Stanley, Keating, and Fox, 1974). The Johns Hopkins programs focus on the early identification and acceleration of very bright children identified largely through conventional tests, but they do not directly attempt to foster creativity.

Perhaps the most that training can accomplish is to facilitate the development of scientific creativity in persons already highly selected on the basis of predisposing factors. This is what ideally happens in superior graduate programs, although the selection process often overemphasizes cognitive abilities and underemphasizes noncognitive, personal characteristics.

4

Child-Rearing Influences on Creativity in Science*

U P TO THIS POINT, we have focused on adult creativity; but because we believe that the childhood experiences of creative persons are of great interest to parents and teachers, we will try here to present the best evidence available on the subject. There have been few studies of the child-rearing experiences of creative adults; therefore, we have broadened our review to include studies using high school and college students. It seems preferable to reach conclusions with limited applicability than to reach no conclusions at all.

We realize that, by considering both adults and students, we are implicitly assuming that real-life creativity has similar antecedents at the auctorive and at the amateur level. This assumption is tentative, but there is some evidence that auctors are likely to emerge from the ranks of young persons showing creativity at the

---

* By the authors in collaboration with Cheryl Hartman.

amateur level (Segal, Busse, and Mansfield, in press). Nevertheless, our conclusions about the child-rearing antecedents of auctorive creativity should be considered more speculative than our conclusions in chapter 3 about the personal characteristics of auctors.

In the studies reviewed here, creativity criteria have generally consisted of ratings by experts, supervisors, and teachers. Studies using divergent thinking or other tests as the only criteria were omitted, because, as we have shown, most of these tests have not given strong and consistent relationships with real-life creative performance.

Data from child-rearing studies have come largely from two sources: (1) scientists or potential scientists themselves; and (2) their parents. Both sources of information may suffer from distortions due to defensiveness, changes in the child-rearing relationship over time, and memory lapses. A number of researchers have dealt with these problems at some length (Burton, 1970; Robbins, 1963; Yarrow, 1963; Yarrow, Campbell, and Burton, 1970).

This chapter is divided into three sections: (1) the parent-child interaction; (2) parent characteristics; and (3) family characteristics. Many studies are encountered repeatedly, as different child-rearing variables are considered. To avoid repetition, some details of the studies, including sample characteristics and creativity criteria, are presented in Table 4.1. As can be seen there, some studies are concerned not only with scientific creativity but also with creativity in other areas. Only those findings pertaining to creativity in science are discussed here. Perhaps because of the paucity of research, few consistent conclusions emerge from studies relating childhood experiences to creativity in nonscientific fields.

THE PARENT-CHILD INTERACTION

In this section, we consider research relating parental child-rearing behaviors to children's creativity. The variables measuring parental child-rearing behaviors in the studies of real-life scientific creativity are: parental autonomy fostering, parental control, parental disciplinary techniques, parental hostility, parental warmth, parental intellectual stimulation, and emotional intensity of parental involvement. Other variables have occasionally been used, but not often in studies involving real-life scientific creativity.

Parental Autonomy Fostering

The autonomy-fostering parent is often thought to be the opposite of the controlling parent, but, as Busse (1967) has shown, this is not always the case. A parent can be at times highly supportive of a child's independence and at other times highly controlling. A parent can even be highly controlling in pushing a child toward independence. Consequently, parental autonomy fostering and parental control are considered separately. Parental autonomy fostering means encouraging a child to act autonomously, independently, or self-reliantly. It is more than the absence of controlling or constricting behavior.

Most research relating parental autonomy fostering to creativity has been conducted with male or mostly male samples. These studies will be considered first.

Three studies (Chambers, 1964, psychologists; Datta and Parloff, 1967; MacKinnon, 1962a, 1968a) found a positive relationship between parental autonomy fostering and creativity, but the Chambers and MacKinnon studies did not differentiate the results according to the sex of the parent. Chambers (1964) found that creative psychologists, more often than the control group members, described their families as individualistic ones in which "each person went his own way." Creative male architects told MacKinnon (1962a, 1968a) that their parents granted them unusual freedom in exploration and decision making. Datta and Parloff (1967) found that scientifically creative male high school seniors more

TABLE 4.1
DETAILS OF CHILD-REARING STUDIES

Studies	Sample	Creativity Variables	Creativity Criteria
Brooks (1963)	45 male industrial research scientists	Creative originality	Ratings by peers, supervisors, and a combination of these two ratings
Chambers (1964)	225 male chemists and 213 male psychologists	Eminence in chemistry; eminence in psychology	National recognition and expert peer judgment
Clark (1957)	639 psychologists receiving doctorates 1930–1944	Significant contributions to psychology	Expert peer ratings
Datta (1967a)	573 male high school seniors	Potential scientific creativity	Ratings by judges in the Westinghouse Science Talent Search
Datta (1967b)	573 male high school seniors	Potential scientific creativity	Ratings by judges in the Westinghouse Science Talent Search
Datta (1968)	573 male high school seniors	Potential scientific creativity	Ratings by judges in the Westinghouse Science Talent Search
Datta and Parloff (1967)	1039 male high school seniors	Potential scientific creativity	Ratings by judges in the Westinghouse Science Talent Search
Drevdahl (1961)	30 psychologists	Creativity	Expert peer ratings

Helson (1971)	41–47 female mathematicians	Mathematical creativity	Expert peer ratings
Helson and Crutchfield (1970)	56–63 male mathematicians	Mathematical creativity	Expert peer nominations
Holland (1961)	649 male and 345 female National Merit Finalists (high school juniors)	Scientific creativity; artistic creativity	Self-report checklists of creative accomplishments
Lehman and Witty (1931)	1,189 scientists	Significant scientific work	Starred in *American Men of Science* (1927), plus miscellaneous criteria
MacCurdy (1956)	406 male and 98 female freshmen and sophomore college students	Potential scientific talent	Science aptitude test, high school record, teacher ratings, student essay, plus interview rating and a social attitudes test
MacKinnon (1961, 1962a, 1968a).	124 male architects	Architectural creativity	Expert peer ratings
Moulin (1955)	164 male chemists, physicists, medical doctors, and physiologists	Major discoveries	Nobel prizes

TABLE 4.1 (cont.)

Studies	Sample	Creativity Variables	Creativity Criteria
Nichols (1964)	796 male and 450 female high school senior National Merit Finalists and their mothers	Scientific achievements; literary achievements	Self-reported creative achievements
Nichols and Holland (1963)	544 male and 275 female National Merit Finalists	Rare scientific achievement, achievement in dramatic activities, rare literary achievement, rare musical achievement, rare achievement in graphic arts, and total artistic achievement reported after the first year of college	Self-report checklists of creative accomplishments
Roe (1951a)	20 male biologists	Eminence in biology	Expert peer ratings plus membership in national honor societies in science
Roe (1951b)	22 male physical scientists	Eminence in physical science	Expert peer ratings plus membership in national honor societies in science

Study	Sample	Criterion	Measure
Roe (1953)	14 male psychologists and 8 male anthropologists	Eminence in psychology or anthropology	Expert peer ratings
Schaefer and Anastasi (1968)	400 male high school students	Scientific and mathematical creativity; literary and graphic arts creativity	Teacher nominations plus Alternate Uses and Consequences tests
Stein (1956, 1962, 1963)	46 male industrial research chemists	Creativity	Supervisors' rankings
D. Taylor (1963)	66 male physicists and 103 male electronics engineers and scientists	For physicists: originality. For engineers and scientists: creativity	Supervisors' ratings
Walberg (1967)	442 male high school physics students	Scientific awards; artistic awards (including performing arts, music, writing, visual arts)	Self-reported recognition, awards, or prizes won
Ypma (1968)	2 samples of 160 chemists or chemical engineers each; 75 miscellaneous scientists	Creativity, productivity	Supervisors' ratings, creative products (e.g., patents, publications), and combination of these

often described their fathers as autonomy fostering than did a less creative group. The two groups did not differ in perceptions of their mothers' autonomy-fostering behavior.

Five studies (Brooks, 1963; Chambers, 1964, chemists; Drevdahl, 1961; Nichols and Holland, 1963; Ypma, 1968) found no relationship between parental autonomy fostering and male creativity. Brooks, using industrial research scientists, found that an "independence in the family" factor did not relate to peers' or supervisors' ratings of creative originality. This factor had high loadings from both mothers' and fathers' emphasis on independence as reported by the scientists. Chambers found that creative and control chemists did not differ in describing their families as individualistic ones in which "each person went his own way." Drevdahl, using small numbers of psychologists, found that creative and control groups did not differ in response to the item labeled "Independence of action was encouraged in childhood and adolescence." Ypma found that two items concerning freedom and independence in childhood did not predict creativity in industrial research scientists. Nichols and Holland, studying National Merit finalists, found no relationship between parental concerns that their children be independent or self-reliant and the students' creative achievements in science.

Only one study related parental autonomy fostering to scientific real-life creativity in females. Nichols and Holland (1963), in their study of National Merit finalists, found no relationship between the fathers' and mothers' concerns that their daughters be independent or self-reliant and the girls' reports of creative achievements in science.

In summary, there is some evidence for a positive relationship between parental encouragement of independence, particularly by fathers, and the development of creativity in boys. One study found that parental encouragement of independence had no effect on girls' creativity.

Parental Control

Parental control has many facets. It can be as direct and simple as a command or as complex and subtle as a negative emotional overtone contradicting the verbal message, "Yes, you may go." Consequently, it is often difficult to decide what research is relevant to parental control and whether studies assessing different kinds of control are really comparable.

A number of studies related parental control and children's scientific creativity. The findings for boys are contradictory, while those for girls consistently show no relationship.

Nichols (1964) found that boys' scientific creativity was positively related to mothers' authoritarian, controlling attitudes; there was no relationship between these variables for girls. Holland (1961) found that the intrusiveness scale of the mother Parental Attitude Research Instrument (PARI) was positively related to scientific achievement in boys but not in girls. The strictness scale and the excluding of outside influences scale were unrelated to scientific creativity for either sex.

Two other studies failed to find a positive relationship between male scientific creativity and parental control. Nichols and Holland (1963) found authoritarian attitudes of both parents were unrelated to "rare scientific achievement" in college students of either sex. Datta and Parloff (1967) found a *negative* relationship between parental control and the scientific creativity of high school boys. Creative boys perceived their fathers to be less authoritarian than did the control group. They perceived both parents to be less controlling and less enforcement-oriented than did the less creative males. No differences were found for such indirect forms of control as possessiveness, overprotection, intrusiveness, and inducement of guilt.

Parental Disciplinary Techniques

Only a few studies directly relate disciplinary techniques to creativity, and little coherence is apparent among the findings. MacKinnon's (1962a, 1968a) creative male architects described their parents' discipline as almost always consistent and predictable. In Drevdahl's (1961) study, a small number of creative psychologists reported that their families used reward rather than punishment more frequently than did a group of noncreative, nonproductive psychologists. No differences were found between the creative psychologists and a noncreative, productive group. Datta and Parloff (1967), in a study of scientifically talented male high school seniors, found creative and comparison groups did not differ in perceptions of their mothers' and fathers' discipline techniques. These three studies provide no evidence for a general relationship between parental disciplinary techniques and creativity.

Parental Hostility

Datta and Parloff (1967), in a study of scientifically talented male high school seniors, used five scales to assess perceptions of parental hostility: rejecting, rejection, hostile control, harsh punishment, and hostile detachment. More and less creative groups did not differ in perception of their fathers, but the more creative group perceived their mothers to be lower in hostile detachment.

Parental Warmth

Parental warmth is treated separately from parental hostility because these two variables, although superficially appearing to be opposites, can be relatively independent of one another (e.g., Busse, 1967).

Three studies relating parental warmth to creativity

have yielded inconsistent results. Helson and Crutch-field (1970) found that creative male mathematicians, when compared with controls, reported having received more affection or attention from their mothers. In contrast, Datta and Parloff (1967) found that creative and less creative high school seniors shared similar perceptions of their parents on three scales related to warmth: affectionate, accepting, and symbolic love reward. Likewise, Brooks (1963) found two factors—mothers' emotional warmth and adjustment and fathers' emotional warmth and adjustment—did not relate to either peers' or supervisors' creative originality ratings for a sample of industrial research scientists. The lack of agreement between these studies may be due to differences in the levels or the fields in which creativity was studied.

Quantity of Parent-Child Interaction

Some parents participate in most of their children's out-of-school activities, whereas other parents limit their interaction to several bland greetings per day. The quantity of parent-child interaction should be distinguished from the quality of the interaction, as well as from the intensity of emotional involvement between parent and child, although it seems likely that there are interactions among these three variables.

Only one study could be located relating scientific creativity to the quantity of parent-child interaction in general. Holland (1961) found no relationship between the "comradeship and sharing" scale of the mother PARI and either sons' or daughters' scientific creativity.

Parental Intellectual Stimulation

Parental intellectual stimulation has shown mixed evidence of a positive relationship with scientific creativity. Drevdahl (1961), using a small number of psychologists, found weak evidence for a positive relationship between parental intellectual stimulation and creativity. A creative group scored higher than one of three overlapping comparison groups on the item labeled, "Major academic stimulation was provided by parents or parental figures other than educators." In contrast, Brooks (1963) found no relationship between a factor entitled "mothers' intellectual emphasis" and peers' or supervisors' ratings for a group of industrial research scientists. The scientists themselves provided the data for assessing their mothers' behavior.

Emotional Intensity of
Parental Involvement

A number of studies show that a low-intensity parent-child relationship may be conducive to the development of creativity in males. Roe (1951a, p. 26) noted "a general dearth of close ties" in her sample of eminent biologists. And in a study of eminent male physical scientists, Roe (1951b) observed that neither great closeness nor serious disagreement was common with either parent during childhood. More creative industrial chemists studied by Stein (1956, 1962, 1963) described themselves as more distant from their mothers and fathers and from adults in general during childhood than did less creative chemists. Finally, MacKinnon (1962a, 1968a) reported that his creative male architects often lacked intense closeness with one or both parents.

In contrast to the studies showing a negative relationship between the intensity of parent-child involvement and male creativity, two studies found some evidence for a positive relationship. Helson and Crutchfield (1970) found that creative male mathematicians, more often than controls, reported a high degree of emotional involvement with their mothers. A small group of creative psychologists studied by Drevdahl (1961) reported a greater attachment to home and family than did one of two very small, overlapping comparison groups.

To summarize, low intensity parent-child relationships seem conducive to creativity in males. It is likely that the relationship between the intensity of the parent-child interaction and creativity is mediated by other variables, such as intellectual stimulation. For example, a close parent-child relationship seems generally detrimental to creativity, but creativity may be enhanced by a close relationship which fosters interest in some intellectual area.

PARENTAL CHARACTERISTICS

Two aspects of parental characteristics have drawn substantial attention: parental child-rearing values, and parental interests. First, parental child-rearing values or attitudes may foster a child's creativity. Hence a number of researchers have focused on parental attitudes about children's autonomy, ambition, and curiosity. A second way in which parents influence their children is by modeling behaviors which are subsequently imitated. Parents' participation in scientific interests or hobbies has been of particular concern here.

Parental Child-Rearing Values

Parents have different views of the ideal child. For example, some parents value autonomy and ambition for their children, whereas others value dependability and popularity.

Of the studies relating parental child-rearing values to creativity, one (MacKinnon, 1962a) involved architects, and two (Holland, 1961; Nichols and Holland, 1963) involved National Merit finalists. MacKinnon reported that the families of creative architects he studied valued integrity, quality, success, ambition, respectability, and intellectual and cultural endeavor.

In two studies (Holland, 1961; Nichols and Holland, 1963), parents of National Merit finalists were asked to rank their preferences for the following characteristics in their children: (1) able to defend himself; (2) ambitious; (3) curious; (4) dependable and reliable; (5) a good student; (6) happy and well-adjusted; (7) independent or self-reliant; (8) popular; and (9) self-controlled.

These rankings, which were completed by fathers in the Holland (1961) study and by both parents in the Nichols and Holland (1963) study, were related to a number of self-report scales completed by the students. The scale most clearly reflecting creative accomplishment in science was called "rare scientific achievement." The most noteworthy finding from these two studies was that fathers who encouraged their daughters' ambition were likely to have scientifically creative daughters. This result is consistent with other findings showing that fathers play the major part in the sex typing of daughters' activities (Lynn, 1974, pp. 140–66). This sex typing often results in scientific pursuits being labeled masculine.

Parental Interests

Do parental interests and hobbies help to explain the development of creativity in children? Parents with many interests, especially intellectual ones, can be expected to expose their children to a wide variety of ideas. Exposure to many ideas and interests should stimulate similar interests in children as well as provide them with a wellspring of information potentially useful in creative endeavors.

Children's scientific creativity may be related to a specific parental interest in science. Schaefer and Anastasi (1968) found that the parents of scientifically creative males were more likely than the parents of a comparison group to have scientific magazines in their homes. The fathers of the creative males had more scientific hobbies; they also had more interests of a conventional nature than did fathers of the comparison boys. The creatives' fathers more often majored in business subjects in college, played bridge as a hobby, and taught their sons about sports.

Shared interests between parent and child may also facilitate creativity in architecture. MacKinnon (1962a) reported that almost without exception one or both parents of his male creative architects were artistically inclined.

A conclusion emerging from these two studies is that children's creativity in an area may be fostered by parental interests in that same area. The fathers of scientifically creative males often had scientific hobbies, and there were often scientific magazines around the homes of scientifically creative males.

FAMILY CHARACTERISTICS

In this section, we consider a number of variables characterizing the families of creative persons. The topics reviewed here are birth order, sibling characteristics, family size, parental absence, social class status, residential location and mobility, and religious background. Other topics for which enticing hypotheses exist (e.g., childhood illness) have not yet spawned sufficient research.

The topics are reviewed with minimal detail because they cannot directly affect the development of creativity; their effect must be mediated by other factors such as parental autonomy fostering behavior and the intensity of parent-child interaction.

Birth Order

Many studies (Chambers, 1964, chemists; Helson and Crutchfield, 1970; Holland, 1961; Roe, 1951a, 1951b, 1953) have shown that first-born males show greater scientific creativity than later-born males. Other studies (Chambers, 1964, psychologists; Datta, 1967a, 1968; Walberg, 1967; Ypma, 1968) found no relationship. Schachter (1963) has argued that the positive relationships can be explained by the disproportionate percentage of first-born sons who attend college and are thus in a position to enter scientific professions. Schachter's argument presents a plausible explanation for Roe's findings, but it cannot explain differences between creative and comparison groups possessing the same level of education (e.g., Chambers, 1964, chemists; Helson and Crutchfield, 1970; Holland, 1961).

Helson (1971), in the only study that could be located

relating birth order and creativity in women, found no relationship.

Family Size

Many studies (Datta, 1967a, 1968; Helson and Crutchfield, 1970; Nichols and Holland, 1963; Roe, 1951a, 1951b, 1953; Walberg, 1967) have investigated the relationship of family size to scientific creativity. None have found any relationship.

Parental Absence

Parental absence is sometimes thought to be a stimulus to creative production (e.g., Eisenstadt, 1978), but the empirical evidence is mixed. The findings of MacKinnon (1961) and Roe (1951a) suggest a relationship between parental absence and creativity, but those of Roe (1951b, 1953) and Donald Taylor (1963) do not.

Social Class

Many studies have related creativity in science to social class variables such as parent education and occupation. A positive relationship has been generally found (e.g., Chambers, 1964; Helson, 1971; Helson and Crutchfield, 1970; Moulin, 1955; Schaefer and Anastasi, 1968; Ypma, 1968; Zuckerman, 1977, p. 64), particularly for males. A few studies (e.g., Brooks, 1963; Clark, 1957; Walberg, 1967) have shown no relationship, but only one study could be located which showed a negative relationship (Stein, 1956). The interaction of socioeconomic status with other variables should be considered in future studies.

Childhood Residence:
Location and Mobility

Two aspects of childhood residence have been studied in relation to creativity: home location (urban, suburban, rural) and residential mobility. Evidence relating creativity to home location is mixed (Datta, 1967b; Helson and Crutchfield, 1970; MacCurdy, 1956; Stein, 1956; Donald Taylor, 1963; Walberg, 1967).

Two studies (MacKinnon, 1962a; Walberg, 1967) found positive relationships between scientific creativity and residential mobility. However, MacCurdy (1956) found that residential mobility during the high school years showed no relationship to creativity.

Religion

Most scientifically creative men do not come from very religious families, and most do not become religiously committed adults (Chambers, 1964; Lehman and Witty, 1931; MacKinnon, 1962a; Roe, 1951a, 1951b, 1953). There is evidence (Arieti, 1976; Clark, 1957; Datta, 1967b; Helson and Crutchfield, 1970; Zuckerman, 1977, p. 68) suggesting that males from Jewish families seem to be extraordinarily creative in science.

CONCLUSIONS

Scientific creativity has shown a number of relationships with family variables, but the paucity of consistent relationships between creativity and parental child-rearing practices is noteworthy. Perhaps parental attitudes and behaviors really do have limited effects on creativity; however, several other interpretations are possible. First, the relationships of creativity to most of the child-rearing variables have been examined in only a small number of studies. Additional research may establish other relationships. Second, as mentioned earlier, the measures used to assess child-rearing practices and attitudes often have questionable validity. Third, since creative scientists vary considerably in their profiles on the personality characteristics, there are likely to be many different possible child-rearing antecedents of auctorive creativity. Most child-rearing antecedents would therefore possess only very small relationships with creativity; such small relationships might prove difficult to establish, given the methodological problems in child-rearing research. It should be noted that our findings pertain only to scientists. In nonscientific fields, creativity may show more relationships to child-rearing variables. However, there are only a handful of studies relating child-rearing practices to auctorive creativity in nonscientific fields.

A fairly clear picture emerges of a few childhood antecedents of scientific creativity in men. Too few studies of women have been made to permit conclusions to be drawn. The scientifically creative man is likely to come from an upper-middle class family in which religion is relatively unimportant. The family is likely to have moved frequently. He is likely to be the first born in his family. His father is likely to have had scientific interests and hobbies. Some intellectual stimulation may have come from his parents. However, the creative man's relationships with his parents were likely to be lacking in emotional closeness. In their child-rearing practices, his parents were likely to encourage independence and autonomy.

Because we have focused on parental child-rearing influences in this chapter, one could erroneously conclude that creativity depends primarily on parental socialization. We believe that the roots of scientific creativity are much more complex. First, the genetic factors that influence intelligence severely limit the number of people who can enter scientific professions and who can thereby have a chance to show scientific creativity. Second, the parent-child interaction is not controlled solely by the parents. Children are apparently born with temperamental characteristics, which even influence their parents' behavior (e.g., Birns, 1965; Brown, 1964; Thomas and Chess, 1977; Thomas, Chess, and Birch, 1970). Third, parents are not the only important agents of socialization: schools and churches, grandparents and peers, as well as other social and cultural factors can influence a child's development of creativity.

Many parents may be interested in applying these

findings to foster creativity in their children, but there are dangers as well as benefits in emphasizing one value to the exclusion of others (Montour, 1977). This point is well expressed by Norbert Weiner (1953), a child prodigy and gifted mathematician, who was not without misgivings about his own parents' successful but highly rigorous fostering of his intellectual development:

What does the sculptor do except remove the surplus marble from the block and make the figure come to life with his own brain and out of his own love? And yet, if the stone be spaulded and flawed, the statue will crumble under the mallet and chisel of the artist. Let those who choose to carve a human soul to their own measure be sure that they have a worthy image after which to carve it, and let them know that the power of molding an emerging intellect is a power of death as well as a power of life. (P. 136)

5

Processes Used by Creative Scientists

CHAPTER 3 DEALT WITH THE characteristics of auctors. To understand why these personal characteristics are important, we must understand the processes used by auctors in their work. Many theories have been developed to explain the creative process. The diverse perspectives of the theories include psychoanalysis (Arieti, 1976; Kris, 1952; Kubie, 1958), Gestalt theory (Köhler, 1969; Wertheimer, 1959), associationism (Mednick, 1962), perception (Schachtel, 1959), humanism (Maslow, 1959, 1967; Rogers, 1959), and cognitive developmental theory (Feldman, 1974). Still other theories combine selected elements from a variety of perspectives (e.g., Gruber, 1974; Hadamard, 1945; Haslerud, 1972; Koestler, 1964). A review of these and other theories can be found elsewhere (Busse and Mansfield, 1980). Our theory differs from most of these in that we focus on creative processes only in scientific fields.

What kinds of studies can be used to gain insights about the processes used by creative scientists? In chapter 3, we argued that the personal characteristics of auctors can be best understood through studies of auctors.

The same argument applies to the processes used by auctors. However, the lack of controlled studies of creative processes used by auctors in scientific fields forces a reliance upon descriptive personal accounts, which are subject to bias and distortion. A scientist may, for example, unconsciously alter his report to make it conform to some view of the scientific method. In one significant case, however, the objection of retrospective bias does not apply. Charles Darwin kept voluminous notebooks in which he recorded his thinking. Because Darwin dated many of the entries in his notebooks, it is possible to follow the course of his thinking.

Since generalizations made from a single case are limited, we also rely on personal accounts by other scientists. Although these accounts are susceptible to distortion and omission, they do show similarities to each other and to the processes revealed in Darwin's notebooks and therefore help to illuminate the processes of scientific creativity.

The scientists considered in this chapter are among the most creative in the history of science; in our terminology, they are at the upper end of the auctorive continuum. Many of the studies reviewed in earlier chapters investigated creativity among more average scientists. Certainly, there are differences between creative geniuses and creative Ph.D.'s in industry or in a university; but it seems reasonable to suppose that the processes they employ are similar.

We shall try to identify several essential processes occurring in the development of auctorive scientific products. These processes do not operate in isolation but rather interact and facilitate each other. Nor do they always occur in the sequence in which they are presented: the mind of the scientist does not usually proceed in an orderly, rational manner.

Examples of the processes will be drawn primarily from accounts of four scientists: James Watson (Olby, 1974; Watson, 1968), who, with two other researchers, was awarded the Nobel prize for discovery of the structure of DNA and the mechanism of genetic transmission; Albert Einstein (Wertheimer, 1959, pp. 213–33), who revolutionized physics with his theory of relativity; Johannes Kepler (Koestler, 1964, pp. 124–30), who showed that planetary orbits are elliptical; and Marie Curie (Curie, 1937), who, with her husband, Pierre, first identified radium and polonium. Following presentation of the processes, we shall illustrate their operation in one of the most detailed accounts available of a scientific discovery—Charles Darwin's thinking that led to his theory of evolution.

SELECTION OF THE PROBLEM

If a scientist is to make a creative breakthrough, he should select a problem that is ready to be solved; the solution must be at least remotely possible, given the instruments, methods, and knowledge available to him. Or, to paraphrase Otto Warburg, research is the art of finding problems that can be solved (Austin, 1978, p. 168). A number of investigators (e.g., Getzels and Csikszentmihalyi, 1975, 1976; Hadamard, 1945; Rokeach, 1965) have emphasized the importance of problem finding or problem selection.

Sometimes the possibility of a creative solution is obvious to an investigator from the outset. James Watson, for example, concentrated on discovering the structure of DNA, because he believed that solution of this problem would reveal the mechanism of genetic transmission. In other cases, a scientist may not be aware of the possibility of a creative outcome at the start of a line of inquiry, but his work is guided by a sensitivity to research findings that present problems for existing theory. Einstein, for example, in the thinking that eventually led to the theory of relativity, noticed that the Newtonian laws governing mechanical processes could not easily be applied to light. Newton had established that there could be no such thing as absolute motion or absolute rest; it seemed clear that the same laws should apply to light. But Einstein noticed that the assumption of a variable velocity of light was incompatible with known electromagnetic phenomena.

Another well-known example of auctorive creativity arising from sensitivity to a problem is the case of Kepler's formulation of elliptical planetary orbits. Kepler was troubled by the fact that the accurate instruments and methods developed by Tycho de Brahe for recording positions of stars and planets had produced data showing that the observed positions of Mars differed by as much as eight minutes of arc from those predicted by the then accepted Ptolemaic theory, which explained the motion of planets by principles based on circular motion. Eventually, Kepler saw that the observed movement of Mars could be explained only by discarding the Ptolemaic belief of motion in perfect circles. When Kepler substituted the notion of oval planetary orbits around the sun, he had to explain the oval shape of the orbits. Since this could be done only by assuming that the orbits resulted from two antagonistic forces, Kepler was led to create a new theory, one which applied the laws of physics to celestial bodies.

In the development of auctorive products, the importance of sensitivity to problems cannot be overemphasized. B. F. Skinner (1959), discussing one of his findings, argues that such sensitivity should guide all scientific research:

> The major result of this experiment was that some of my rats had babies. I began to watch young rats. I saw them right themselves and crawl about very much like the decerebrate or thalamic cats and rabbits of Magnus. So I set about studying the postural reflexes of young rats. Here was a first principle not formally recognized by scientific methodologists: when you run onto something interesting, drop everything else and study it. (P. 363)

Such serendipitous events leading to the selection of important problems are apparently quite common (e.g., Austin, 1978; Barber and Fox, 1962; Cannon, 1945, pp. 68–78; Merton, 1968, pp. 157–62; Rosner and Abt, 1972, pp. 7–25).

It is likely that sensitivity in the selection of research problems is a primary factor differentiating auctorive scientists from less creative ones.

Extended Effort to Solve a Problem

Creative accomplishments in science do not come easily. In the case of a major discovery, there is almost always an extended period of persistent effort before a solution begins to emerge. Francis Crick and James Watson, for example, spent a year and a half trying to discover the structure of DNA before developing the model that won them a Nobel prize. Einstein spent seven years working on the problem of the velocity of light in relation to different frames of reference before he hit upon the key to the solution and developed his theory of special relativity. Many other examples of persistent effort could be mentioned. The amount of effort and time required in this phase of the creative process varies within wide limits, but it is probably great enough to deter all but the most highly motivated scientists.

One reason for the importance of a period of extended effort is that it increases the likelihood that chance associations will provide clues to the solution of the problem. Austin (1978) observes that chance sometimes operates as a result of a scientist's general exploratory behavior. The scientist who is persistent in investigating a problem is more likely to be the beneficiary of chance. Austin also proposes that chance favors the prepared mind. The importance of the period of extended effort may be to heighten the scientist's receptivity to ideas or associations that are not obviously related to the problem but provide important clues to its solution.

SETTING CONSTRAINTS ON
THE SOLUTION OF THE PROBLEM

In the period of extended effort to solve the problem, the scientist adopts a number of constraints on the problem's solution. A constraint can be broadly conceived as any mental set which limits the scope within which the inquiry is conducted. Constraints can be classified as empirical, theoretical, and methodological. Some constraints are present initially; others are added as new insights develop.

Empirical Constraints

The most obvious type of constraint is imposed by experimental observations or results. Marie Curie, in her study of radioactivity, found that samples of pitchblende produced far more radiation than could be explained by the quantities of uranium and thorium present. Since uranium and thorium were the only two known radioactive elements, this finding led to the search for new elements. For Einstein the most important empirical constraint in the work leading to the theory of relativity was the Michelson-Morely finding, which suggested that the speed of light was independent of any particular frame of reference. Finally, consider the influence on Kepler of Tycho de Brahe's observations showing that the orbit of Mars failed, by up to eight minutes of arc, to conform to predictions based on the Ptolemaic theory of circular planetary motion. Although this discrepancy was small, it could not be ignored, for Tycho de Brahe had developed highly precise methods for observing the heavens.

Empirical findings, especially when they differ from theoretical predictions, probably constitute the single most important type of constraint. Indeed, an essential aspect of the creative process is to recognize which empirical findings are especially important and to plan one's inquiry accordingly. In this sense, the setting of a constraint is closely related to the process of selecting a problem.

Theoretical Constraints

Constraints of this type are adopted with varying degrees of commitment. The theoretical constraints most tenaciously held are likely to be the central assumptions of a theory. Theoretical constraints of this type are similar to what Thomas Kuhn calls paradigms. Kuhn (1970, p. viii) defines paradigms as "universally recognized scientific achievements that for a time provide model problems and solutions to a community of practitioners." Because theoretical assumptions are often widely accepted, a scientist may be unaware that they are constraints. Einstein, for example, initially accepted the prevailing assumption that time was independent of physical processes and could be analyzed independent of any specific frame of reference. It was not until he questioned this constraint that he was able to develop his theory of relativity. Similarly, Kepler at first accepted the Ptolemaic assumption that planetary movement could be explained in terms of the simultaneous operation of circular components of motion. This constraint, like Einstein's initial assumption about time, proved wrong.

Other theoretical constraints, which we call "working hypotheses," are adopted more tentatively. Working hypotheses may be borrowed from other investigators, but often they are adopted by the investigator himself. For example, James Watson, who discovered the structure of DNA and the mechanism of genetic transmission, adopted the working hypothesis that DNA had a helical structure. Watson was influenced by Linus Pauling's demonstration of a helical structure in a protein molecule, as well as by his own demonstration of the helical structure of the tobacco mosaic virus. Eventually, improved X-ray diffraction data confirmed the working hypothesis and elevated it to the status of an empirical constraint.

Methodological Constraints

A third class of constraints, methodological ones, pertain to instrumentation, research strategy, and statistical analysis. The constraints imposed by instruments for obtaining data can be appreciated by considering the tremendous advances that have followed the development of new instruments such as the electron microscope in biology, the cyclotron in physics (Libby, 1970), and the radio telescope in astronomy (Edge and Mulkay, 1976).

The scientist's strategy for obtaining data is another methodological constraint. Its importance is illustrated in James Watson's (1968) account of his work on the structure of DNA. Watson adopted the technique of molecular model building because of the success Linus Pauling had achieved using this technique to discover the structure of another protein molecule:

> The key to Linus' success was his reliance on the simple laws of structural chemistry. The α(alpha)-helix had not been found by only staring at X-ray pictures; the essential trick, instead, was to ask which atoms like to sit next to each other. In place of pencil and paper, the main working tools were a set of molecular models superficially resembling the toys of preschool children. (Watson, 1968, p. 50)

Despite Pauling's success, the technique of model building was not accepted by everyone. Another researcher, Rosalind Franklin, sought to decipher DNA through the analysis of X-ray diffraction patterns of crystallized samples of DNA.

Other methodological constraints are found in the statistical techniques for analyzing data. In the past thirty years, many new statistical techniques have been developed that allow highly complex analyses of data. In the social sciences, for example, techniques such as multiple regression, factor analysis, and multivariate analysis of variance have begun to revolutionize research.

The development of new statistical techniques has been facilitated by the computer. A relatively simple factor analysis that would take months to compute by hand can be accomplished in minutes by a computer.

Summary

We have identified three types of constraints: empirical, theoretical, and methodological. Some constraints, such as major empirical findings, central theoretical assumptions, and available instrumentation, cannot be ignored by the researcher. Other constraints, however, such as empirical findings in related fields, working hypotheses, and research strategies, must be discovered or selected. The choice of initial constraints is extremely important. It is almost inevitable that some initially adopted constraints will prove wrong; but errors in selection must be minimized. The working hypotheses must conform to all relevant empirical findings, and the methodology used must be capable of providing a solution.

CHANGING THE CONSTRAINTS

In the process of developing a scientific accomplishment, it is likely that some initially adopted constraints will prove wrong and will need to be changed. The process of changing constraints is similar to what Philip Jackson and Samuel Messick (1967) call transformation and what the Gestalt psychologists (e.g., Wertheimer, 1959) call restructuring.

Constraints in the form of working hypotheses are relatively easy to break, because they are deliberately adopted and are not part of a much larger system of beliefs. Working hypotheses may be discarded because newly discovered data make them untenable. For example, Watson found that his early model of DNA, which placed the sugar-phosphate backbone in the center of the helix rather than on the outside, was incompatible with the dual constraints imposed by the laws of structural chemistry and the X-ray diffraction patterns revealed in photographs of DNA. When Watson was made aware of these problems, he shifted to a new working hypothesis and began to build models with an exterior backbone.

But constraints based on the central assumptions of a theory or paradigm (Kuhn, 1970) are much more difficult to change. Einstein worked for seven years on the problem of the velocity of light before breaking the constraint of traditional scientific theory regarding time. Breaking the constraints of a paradigm is probably impossible for many people. Thomas Kuhn (1970, p. 90) points out that paradigm change is most often achieved by men who are either very young or very new to a field and thus are not as strongly committed to existing paradigms.[1]

The decision to break a constraint of a paradigm is often preceded by a long period of reluctance. Arthur Koestler (1964) cogently documents Kepler's reluctance to accept the idea of elliptical planetary orbits, although we need not accept his contention that the idea sprang from unconscious sources:

> Kepler, too, nearly threw away the elliptic orbits; for almost three years he held the solution in his hands—without seeing it. His conscious mind refused to accept the "cartload of dung" which the underground had cast up. When the battle was over, he confessed: "Why should I mince my words? The truth of Nature, which I had rejected and chased away, returned by stealth through the backdoor, disguising itself to be accepted. Ah, what a foolish bird I have been!" (P. 217)

What makes a scientist decide to abandon the constraints of a paradigm? For one thing, there is generally significant experimental evidence which violates theoretical predictions and thus is not easily explained

---

1. Note that even relatively young scientists have completed a doctorate or the equivalent and thus have undergone extensive training.

within the context of existing theory. In Einstein's case, this evidence was the Michelson-Morely experiment, while for Kepler it was the observed motion of Mars.

But the existence of such evidence is rarely sufficient to force the change of a paradigm. Almost any data can be made to appear consistent with a theory, provided that new assumptions are added to that theory. Consider the reaction of many physicists to the Michelson-Morely results, which were incompatible with the prediction of existing theory that the velocity of light would vary as a function of its direction with respect to the movement of the earth. Two of Einstein's contemporaries, Lorentz and Fitzgerald, postulated that the measurement apparatus contracted in the direction of the earth's motion. Although Einstein later demonstrated that this formulation was correct, he felt it had an ad hoc quality: no satisfactory explanation was provided for the hypothesized contraction. Nevertheless, the example illustrates the tendency of scientists to cling to an existing paradigm rather than to attempt to create a new one.

In addition to new data, an acceptable alternative theory may be necessary if the constraints of a paradigm are to be changed. Kuhn (1970, p. 77) makes the point that the scientific community never rejects a paradigm unless a plausible alternative is available.

But it is not easy to develop an alternative paradigm or theory. To do so requires viewing the problem from a perspective radically different from those generally used in the field. The accomplishment of this transformation or restructuring is not easy to explain. It seems to require two of the processes already discussed: extended effort, and sensitivity in selection of problems. The full complexity of the problem must be understood, and the most troublesome areas for existing theory must be pinpointed. Detecting troublesome areas is not always easy; it took Einstein a long time to realize that the Michelson-Morely experiment, which had seemed clear in every respect but its result, was really unclear in one crucial respect: the measurement of time. Systematic analysis of the meaning of simultaneity demonstrated to Einstein that the assumption that time could be measured independently of the observer's frame of reference was false. This was the crucial insight that led to a restructuring of traditional notions about space and movement and permitted Einstein to develop the theory of relativity.

Extended effort and sensitivity to problems may sometimes be sufficient by themselves to bring about restructuring. But another technique may also play a facilitating role: breaking away from the problem.

Many creative scientists have reported hitting upon a solution after having put the problem aside for a time. Sometimes the solution seemed to emerge suddenly and without any conscious precipitating association. The mathematician Poincaré (Ghiselin, 1952) describes such an experience:

> Then I turned my attention to the study of some arithmetical questions apparently without much success and without a suspicion of any connection with my preceding researches. Disgusted with my failure, I went to spend a few days at the seaside and thought of something else. One morning, walking on the bluff, the idea came to me, with just the same characteristics of brevity, suddenness, and immediate certainty, that the arithmetic transformations of indeterminate ternary quadratic forms were identical with those of non-Euclidean geometry. (P. 26)

In other cases, the solution or restructuring is triggered by an association with some apparently unrelated thought. In either case, the solution or restructuring comes during a period when the scientist is not consciously trying to solve the problem. But why should putting aside a problem facilitate restructuring?

Arthur Koestler (1964), Henri Poincaré (Ghiselin, 1952), and Jacques Hadamard (1945) assume that unconscious processes are at work, but it is not necessary to attribute a unique creative role to unconscious processes. There is no question that unconscious processes can facilitate restructuring, as when, for example, an image from a dream suggests a new way of looking at a problem. But this does not mean that dreams or other unconscious processes hold the master key to creative thinking. We believe that Howard Gruber's (1974) view is more plausible:

> The usual view of unconscious processes is that they express the way in which a person is divided against himself. But a person is not always so divided. When he bends all his efforts toward some great goal, the same problems which occupy his rational, waking thoughts will shape his imagery and pervade his dreams. (P. 246)

From our standpoint, breaking away from a problem allows a scientist to reapproach a problem with thoughts less dominated by the unproductive constraints which have hindered restructuring in the first place; it also allows him to think in an undirected fashion so that he is open to facilitating associations from random thoughts. In the latter case, a potentially useful idea will trigger analysis through directed thinking.

Chance often plays a key role in the changing of constraints. It may be through chance that the scientist is exposed to the idea or evidence which leads to a restructuring of the problem. As Austin (1978) points out, however, chance does not always operate independently of the scientist's behavior. The scientist who persistently attacks the problem from a variety of directions is likely to do something by chance that leads to the solution of the problem; and the scientist who has had extensive training and experience with a problem is highly sensitive to chance associations and facts that, though apparently unrelated to the problem, are in reality clues to its solution. In difficult problems, the critical associations may come from nonscientific areas, such as hobbies. In such cases, chance favors the scientist with a distinctive life-style and highly personalized nonscientific activities.

VERIFICATION AND ELABORATION

The process of formulating new constraints and testing them is repeated until, by successive approximations, the scientist constructs a set of constraints leading to an acceptable solution. If the solution involves a major restructuring of the field or the introduction of a new paradigm, he must show that it provides a solution to the problems that plague the old paradigm, that it leads to an understanding of other problems not directly related to the scientist's original concern, and that it suggests promising new lines of inquiry.

The time spent on these processes may be relatively short—as in the case of Einstein, who took only five weeks to develop his theory of special relativity after his initial insight into the meaning of time and simultaneity—or much longer—as in the case of Marie Curie, who worked for four years to isolate radium after she had first tentatively identified it as a new element. The processes of verification and elaboration are necessary for a new idea to gain acceptance by the scientific community.

A DETAILED EXAMPLE OF CREATIVE PROCESSES: DARWIN'S DEVELOPMENT OF THE THEORY OF EVOLUTION

The processes of scientific creativity may be better understood by considering a single scientific accomplishment in some detail. For this purpose, we have reserved a highly detailed account: Darwin's development of the theory of evolution through natural selection. We acknowledge our debt to Howard Gruber (1974) for his careful analysis of Darwin's notebooks.

Darwin's selection of the problem of evolution can be traced to his voyage on the *Beagle* to South America and the Galapagos Islands from 1831 to 1836, but his interest in evolution developed gradually and was the product of a number of different influences. During the voyage, Darwin recorded many thousands of notes. Among the phenomena he noticed was the tremendous variability of species; within an island group, slight variations of species could be observed from one island to the next. However, he was not struck by the evolutionary significance of these differences until after the end of his voyage, for, while at sea, he was primarily concerned with geological matters. Geology in Darwin's time was riven by a conflict between those seeking to reconcile geological evidence with the biblical account of the creation and those seeking to explain the same evidence through a process of evolution governed by natural laws. Darwin followed this controversy and was gradually won over to the evolutionary viewpoint. But accepting this viewpoint created a conflict with his view that organisms lived in a stable, harmonious natural order:

> As he came to accept modern geological views of a constantly changing order in the physical world, a contradiction within his point of view developed as follows: each species was adapted to its milieu; the milieu was undergoing constant change; and yet the species were changeless. (Gruber, 1974, p. 20)

Darwin's Selection of the Problem of Evolution

Ten months after the *Beagle* docked in England, Darwin began his "transmutation" notebooks. From this point on, his goal was to develop a theory to explain evolution. At the same time, however, he believed that the concept of evolution would explain many phenomena relating to the geographic distribution of the species and the taxonomic relationships among them. Thus, Darwin's evolving geological views, as well as his naturalistic observations during the voyage of the *Beagle,* sensitized him to problems which existing biological theory could not adequately explain. Darwin's desire to develop a theory of evolution became the "ruling passion" that guided a diverse set of research enterprises (Gruber, 1974, p. 251).

Constraints on Darwin's Thinking

We turn now to a consideration of the constraints set by Darwin in his theory-building. Among the most important were those related to empirical observations. A theory of evolution would have to explain the tremendous variability of species and the existence of very similar species in neighboring geographical regions. Two additional empirical constraints were the geological evidence for an evolving world and the fossil evidence showing that many species had become extinct. These four empirical constraints implied evolution of the species and guided Darwin's earliest attempts to develop a theory of evolution. Later on, he encountered other empirical evidence to which he also adapted his thinking.

Theoretical constraints were also important in guiding Darwin's theory building. Certainly, Darwin's thinking was not limited by the constraints of a scientific paradigm, since prior to Darwin's time, no scientific paradigm governing either evolution or the variability of species existed. Although a few biologists had speculated about evolution, there was no satisfactory theory to explain it; and the biblical story of the creation remained prominent.

Nevertheless, Darwin's thinking was constrained by a number of theoretical concepts or schemes, which we would classify as working hypotheses. Gruber (1974, pp. 117–28) identifies three schemes. The first is the image of the irregularly branching "Tree of Nature," which Darwin used to explain the relationships among species, living and extinct. Another, the "conservation scheme," appears in various guises in Darwin's thought. In his first theory of evolution, later discarded, Darwin assumed that the number of extant species must remain approximately the same. This assumption, coupled with the evidence for extinction of species, led Darwin to believe that new species must constantly be emerging to take the place of those becoming extinct. A third theoretical constraint, identified by Gruber as the "equilibration scheme," refers to the principle that organisms adapt to environmental change.

Another more tentatively held working hypothesis was Darwin's first evolutionary theory, the theory of monads, which was elaborated in his notebooks during July of 1837 (Gruber, 1974, pp. 136–37). This theory held that simple living particles, or monads, are constantly springing into life from inanimate matter as a result of unknown natural forces. In response to physical changes in the environment, the monads evolve, developing into ever more complex forms. Darwin believed that monads, like individual organisms, had a fixed life span and would eventually die. The monad theory was a constraint that Darwin maintained for only a few weeks.

Just as empirical and theoretical constraints guided Darwin's thinking, so did methodological ones. Darwin's research strategy is a prime example. For a long time, Darwin believed that he could not develop a satisfactory theory of evolution until he could explain the wide variability among species (Gruber, 1974, pp. 159–61). This research strategy was a methodological constraint which had to be modified before the development of a satisfactory theory was possible.

Darwin's Changing of Constraints

Darwin's thinking reflected changes in both theoretical and methodological constraints. Let us consider first the changing of a theoretical constraint—Darwin's abandonment of the monad theory. The monad theory (Gruber, 1974, pp. 129–49) had been adopted to explain the existence of simple, one-celled organisms. It was believed that these organisms would have evolved into more complex forms if they had been created long ago. Empirical evidence may have caused the monad theory to be discarded, for Darwin became aware of the work of Ehrenberg, which demonstrated the existence of fossilized unicellular animals identical to existing ones (Gruber, 1974, p. 153). Darwin realized that, if such simple animals had lived unchanged for tens of thousands of years, it was unnecessary to assume, as the monad theory did, that any simple organism must have arisen through recent spontaneous generation. Also, the assumption of a fixed life span for each monad led to the prediction that many species related to the same monad should die out simultaneously; but the available evidence clearly did not support this prediction.

Presumably, these problems caused Darwin to give up the monad theory; but the changing of this theoretical constraint may also have been facilitated by breaking away from the problem, for the monad theory disappeared from Darwin's notes following a four-week vacation.

The most famous example of constraint-changing in Darwin's thinking occurred at the time of his so-called "Malthusian insight." After about two years of searching for an explanation for evolution, Darwin read the *Essay on Population,* in which Thomas Malthus argued that population growth is geometrical, tempered only by factors such as disease and war, which lead to the elimination of maladaptive variants. Darwin's insight was that natural selection could also have a *positive* influence, favoring the occasional variants which were better adapted to the environmental conditions under which they must survive (Gruber, 1974, p. 105).

To arrive at this theory of evolution, Darwin had to modify several constraints. First, he had to recognize the Malthusian principle of superfecundity as a central theoretical constraint. Before this could be done, he had to abandon the monad theory, which assumed constant spontaneous generation of organisms, a superfecund alternative to the Malthusian superfecundity principle (Gruber, 1974, p. 105). The availability of new empirical data showing the dramatic rate of reproduction of microorganisms also helped to prepare Darwin to appreciate the importance of Malthusian superfecundity.

Darwin also had to modify a second constraint, a methodological one. In formulating a research strategy, he had assumed that a theory of evolution had to explain the ubiquitous variation of organisms. Darwin came to realize both that variation alone would not explain evolution and that a viable theory of evolution could be constructed with variation as an unexplained premise. These realizations were facilitated by Darwin's growing awareness of the sheer quantity of variation in nature and his doubts that variation was always adaptive (Gruber, 1974, pp. 159–61).

Once the principles of superfecundity and variation were firmly established as constraints, Darwin was able to appreciate the positive role of natural selection. His familiarity with artificial selection through domestic breeding may have sensitized him to this possibility.

The Malthusian insight resulted from the joint modification of several different constraints. Gruber has suggested reasons for Darwin's modification of these constraints, but it seems unlikely that Darwin would have succeeded in changing these constraints and arriving at his Malthusian insight if he had not had the overriding goal of explaining evolution. Extended effort characterized all of Darwin's work, both before and after the Malthusian insight. Indeed, the processes of verification and elaboration of the theory occupied most of the remaining years of Darwin's professional career. Darwin did not publish his theory of evolution until 1859, more than twenty years after the Malthusian insight.

CONCLUSIONS

We have proposed that five processes are central to the development of auctorive accomplishments in scientific fields: (1) selection of the problem; (2) extended, directed effort; (3) setting constraints; (4) changing constraints; and (5) verification and elaboration.

Our view departs significantly from the assumption that creative products are developed primarily through divergent thinking processes (e.g., Denny, 1968; Torrance, 1962, 1965; Wallach and Kogan, 1965). Accounts of the development of auctorive scientific products do not support the image of the creative scientist as a person who tries to generate many different ideas in the hope that one of them will prove useful. As neurologist James Austin (1978) wrote, "Sensing which ideas to ignore is probably more important than generating many of them" (p. 168).

The processes that we propose are much more convergent and deductive. The creative scientist is guided by empirical, theoretical, and methodological constraints which enormously narrow the range of acceptable new ideas. The processes of setting and changing constraints control the ideas which the scientist generates. The one aspect of divergent thinking which seems potentially important is flexibility of thinking, which might facilitate the changing of constraints.

6

Scientific Creativity: Summary and Synthesis

IN THIS SECTION, we shall integrate conclusions from the previous chapters. First, however, let us briefly summarize these conclusions.

In chapter 1, we argued that creativity should be studied directly: creative persons must be identified on the basis of real-life products or performance, not on the basis of test scores. This argument was advanced on the logical grounds that test performance can be influenced by many factors unrelated to real-life creativity. Moreover, as is evident from the studies reviewed in chapter 2, no existing creativity test even comes close to achieving a one-to-one relationship with real-life creativity in scientists. Indeed, there is very little evidence in scientific areas for the criterion-related validity of most widely used creativity tests, especially those designed to measure divergent thinking abilities.

Therefore, we decided to focus on studies of persons who had demonstrated real-life creativity. Those whose products are judged creative when compared with those of adult professionals we defined as auctors; those whose products are judged creative when compared with those of persons at a nonprofessional level we defined as amateur creatives. We recognize there are large gradations within both levels. For example, it is clear that Watson and Darwin showed far higher levels of creativity than many scientists who were judged creative in various studies reviewed in this book. We decided to focus as much as possible on auctors, who are creative according to a more stringent definition.

In chapter 2, we reviewed studies relating scientific creativity to performance on a variety of tests. This evidence, together with evidence from biographical inventories and informal observations by researchers who have studied auctors, was used in chapter 3 to identify the personal characteristics of creative scientists. Three characteristics common to almost all scientists are regarded as prerequisites for a scientific career: high intelligence, extensive training in a field, and at least moderate emotional adjustment. Beyond these prerequisites are some characteristics which distinguish creative scientists from their less creative peers: autonomy, personal flexibility and openness to experience, need to be original and novel, need for professional recognition, commitment to work, and aesthetic sensitivity. We believe that the latter group of characteristics all contribute to the development of creativity; creative scientists must be generally high on these personal characteristics. Low levels on one or two of the personal characteristics can occur, but they must be compensated for by unusually high levels on other characteristics.

Chapter 4 reviewed the literature on child-rearing antecedents of creativity. Due to the limited number of child-rearing studies of adult scientists, studies involving scientifically creative high school and college students were also considered. The variables relating to the parent-child interaction are of primary importance to the development of creativity. Of these, three showed some indication of a relationship with creativity: low emotional intensity in the parent-child relationship, parental autonomy fostering, and parental intellectual stimulation.

In chapter 5, we developed a theory of the creative process in science. Five processes were identified: (1) selection of the problem; (2) extended effort to solve the problem; (3) setting constraints on the solution of the problem; (4) changing the constraints; and (5) verification and elaboration. These processes are believed to be interactive and overlapping.

A SYNTHESIS

Our conclusions fall into three areas: developmental antecedents of scientific creativity, personal characteristics of creative scientists, and processes used by creative scientists. Our hypotheses about links among these areas are summarized in Figures 6.1 through 6.5. In each of these figures, the column headings and boxes are identical. The selection of the items appearing in the boxes under each heading requires some explanation.

Under "developmental antecedents" are the experiences found to characterize auctors and amateur creatives in science. The three child-rearing variables have already been mentioned. The importance of an apprenticeship with an auctor was discussed in chapter 3.

Some family characteristics were not listed under developmental antecedents because their effects on auctorive personal characteristics are indirect. These omitted characteristics are probably related to the child-rearing antecedents which do appear in Figures 6.1–6.5. For example, the relationship of birth order to scientific creativity can be explained in terms of the greater amounts of stimulation which first-born children often receive from their parents. Low family-religiosity is probably linked to parental autonomy fostering, as is middle-class socio-economic status (e.g., Busse and Busse,

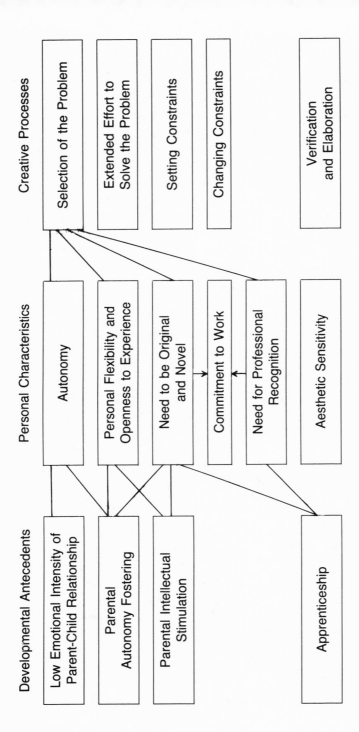

FIGURE 6.1. SELECTION OF THE PROBLEM: LINKS TO PERSONAL CHARACTERISTICS AND DEVELOPMENTAL ANTECEDENTS.

These links pertain to professionals in scientific fields. Personal attributes such as high intelligence, extensive training, and moderate socio-emotional adjustment are not included. Genetic factors are omitted, although they certainly play a role, especially with regard to high ability. Nor are situational factors included, although they interact with personal characteristics to influence the creative processes.

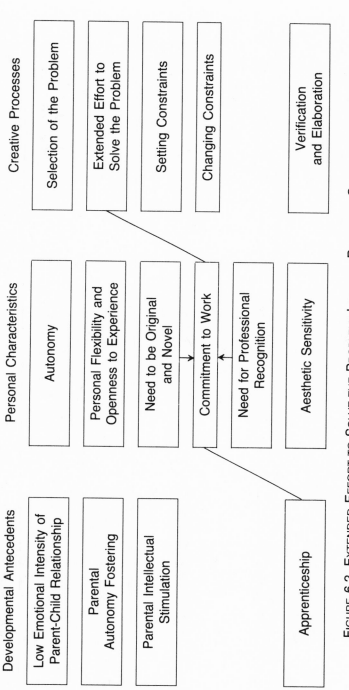

FIGURE 6.2. EXTENDED EFFORT TO SOLVE THE PROBLEM: LINKS TO PERSONAL CHARACTERISTICS AND DEVELOPMENTAL ANTECEDENTS.

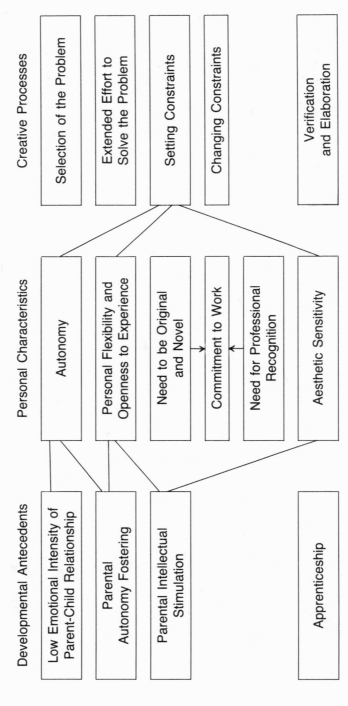

FIGURE 6.3. SETTING CONSTRAINTS: LINKS TO PERSONAL CHARACTERISTICS AND DEVELOPMENTAL ANTECEDENTS.

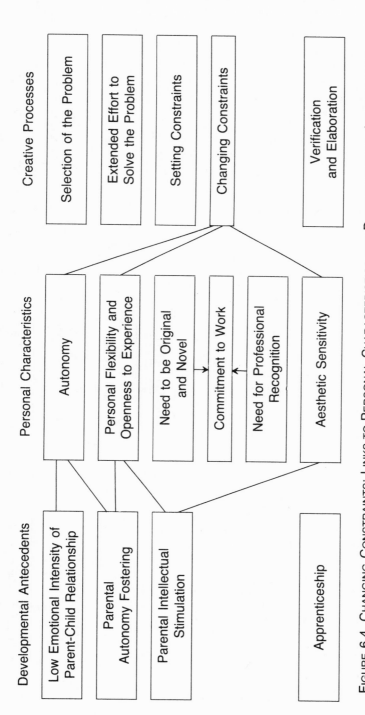

FIGURE 6.4. CHANGING CONSTRAINTS: LINKS TO PERSONAL CHARACTERISTICS AND DEVELOPMENTAL ANTECEDENTS.

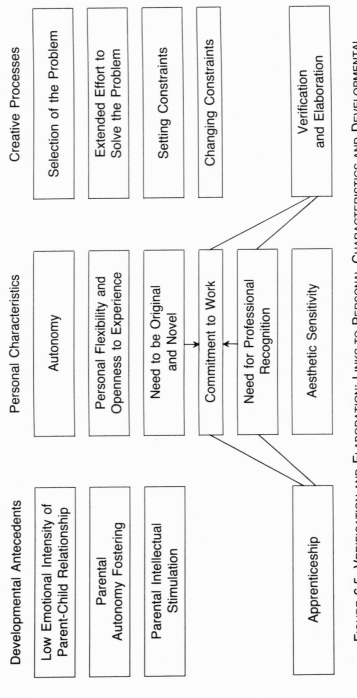

FIGURE 6.5. VERIFICATION AND ELABORATION: LINKS TO PERSONAL CHARACTERISTICS AND DEVELOPMENTAL ANTECEDENTS.

1972). Middle-class status is also undoubtedly related to parental intellectual stimulation. Parents' interests are probably reflected in their intellectual stimulation.

The boxes under the heading "personal characteristics" contain the characteristics differentiating auctors from less creative scientists. The three characteristics that we view as preconditions for professional attainment—above average intelligence, extensive training in a field, and emotional adjustment—were omitted because they are assumed to characterize all scientists. Above average intelligence and extensive training in a field would probably facilitate all of the creative processes.

Notice that under the "personal characteristics" heading, three motivational characteristics are linked. Among auctors, commitment to work can be seen as a partial outcome of high levels of the need to be original and novel and the need for professional recognition.

Figures 6.1–6.5 show links between a creative process and the personal characteristics which facilitate it. These personal characteristics are in turn linked to developmental antecedents. These links pertain to professionals in scientific fields. Just as the figures do not show our three preconditions for professional attainment, genetic factors are likewise omitted, although they certainly play a role, especially with regard to high ability. Nor are situational factors (e.g., working conditions) included, although they probably interact with personal characteristics to influence the creative processes.

Figure 6.1 focuses on the first creative process, selection of the problem. The personal characteristics which most directly facilitate selection of the problem are the need to be original and novel and the need for professional recognition. A prospective auctor must select a problem of sufficient importance that the solution would constitute a creative accomplishment worthy of recognition by others in the field.

Other personal characteristics that may facilitate selection of the problem are autonomy, personal flexibility, and openness to experience. Autonomy is necessary if the problem is not one that has captured the attention of other researchers in the field. Personal flexibility and openness to experience may provide a sensitivity to problems by bringing to the scientist's attention findings from other fields that do not agree with the predictions of theory in his own field.

Figure 6.1 also shows hypothetical links between the personal characteristics already discussed and the developmental antecedents. Autonomy, for example, is most clearly related to parental autonomy fostering, but it might also be fostered by low emotional intensity in the parent-child relationship. Personal flexibility and openness to experience are hypothesized to have roots in parental artistic and intellectual stimulation and also in parental autonomy fostering (e.g., Busse, 1969).

The need to be original and novel probably stems from parental autonomy fostering and parental intellectual stimulation. But this need probably crystallizes as a result of identification with an auctor during an apprenticeship. In a similar way, need for professional recognition also develops during the apprenticeship.

Figure 6.2 shows links to the second creative process—extended effort to solve the problem. Obviously, the personal characteristics of commitment to work will facilitate the process of extended effort that is needed to make auctorive breakthroughs. As was mentioned earlier, commitment to work occurs when the need to be original and novel and the need for professional recognition are high. It is probably developed in conjunction with these two needs during the apprenticeship.

Figure 6.3 shows links to the process of setting constraints. The personal characteristics most likely to facilitate setting constraints are personal flexibility and openness to experience. For example, openness may mean that the scientist becomes aware of findings outside of his own field that can serve as empirical constraints. Flexibility and openness, as well as autonomy, make it easier for the scientist to adopt new or different methodologies, which also serve as constraints.

The changing of constraints is the focus of Figure 6.4. The links are identical to those in Figure 6.3. Autonomy is essential to the changing of constraints, especially widely accepted theoretical and methodological ones. Personal flexibility and openness to experience will also facilitate the changing of constraints, since these characteristics make the scientist aware of findings that do not fit the theoretical constraints which have already been set. Aesthetic sensitivity may also facilitate the changing of constraints, especially when the scientist is "blocked" after a period of extended effort. Many ideas or associations to the problem will occur, but most will not be analyzed in detail. However, those ideas with aesthetic appeal, by virtue of simplicity or elegance, are likely to trigger direct, logical analysis.

Figure 6.5 focuses on the creative process of verification and elaboration. This process, like the period of extended effort to solve the problem, depends on a high level of commitment to work. It is also linked to the need for professional recognition, since there is little recognition until a discovery has been verified and elaborated.

Appendix A

Criterion-related Validity of Cognitive and Perceptual Tests

FOUR OF THESE TESTS, WHICH showed at least some promise as predictors of creativity in scientific fields, are reviewed in chapter 2. The remaining tests are reviewed in this appendix. See chapter 2 for an overall discussion. Under each test, studies are reviewed alphabetically by author.

Throughout this appendix, all subscales that showed significant relationships with the creativity criteria will be noted. The remaining subscales mentioned by the researchers showed nonsignificant relationships.

TESTS REVIEWED IN THIS APPENDIX

Apparatus Test
Concept Mastery Test
Consequences Test
Gestalt Completion Test
Gestalt Transformation Test
Gottschaldt Figures Test
Ideational Fluency Test
Match Problems Test
Pertinent Questions Test
Social Institutions Test
Unusual Uses Test
Wechsler Adult Intelligence Scale
Word Association Test

Apparatus Test

The Apparatus Test requires a subject to suggest two improvements for each of twenty common appliances and implements (e.g., telephone, safety razor).

Mullins (1959) found that four scores from the Apparatus Test were not significantly related to supervisors' ratings of creativity in a sample of 131 research scientists in various fields.

Calvin Taylor and his co-workers (Taylor and Ellison, 1964; Taylor, Smith, Ghiselin, and Ellison, 1961) also found that Apparatus Test scores were not related significantly to any of three creativity criteria for 107 physical scientists. The three criteria were supervisory ratings of creativity and factors titled "creativity rating by laboratory chiefs" and "originality of written work."

It is doubtful that the Apparatus Test will prove of much value in measuring scientific creativity.

Concept Mastery Test

The Concept Mastery Test is a high-level test of the ability to deal with verbal concepts and abstractions. This untimed test consists of synonym-antonym items and both verbal and numerical analogies.

Gough (1961), in a study of forty-five industrial research scientists, found the Concept Mastery Test was not significantly related to a creativity criterion derived from equally weighted peer and supervisors' ratings of creativity.

Helson (1961, 1971), using forty-four female mathematicians, found a significant positive correlation between the Concept Mastery Test and creativity ratings made by other mathematicians.

MacKinnon (1962b) reported a nonsignificant correlation between expert ratings of creativity and the Concept Mastery Test among forty creative male architects. It should be noted, however, that the creative architects were all of high intelligence.

McDermid (1965) found the total score from the Concept Mastery Test was significantly related to peer ratings but not to supervisors' ratings of creativity for an educationally heterogeneous group of fifty-eight male engineers and technical personnel.

Donald Taylor (1963) reported the Concept Mastery Test was not significantly correlated with supervisors' ratings of creativity in a sample of about 103 men who were mostly electronics engineers and electronics scientists.

Some negative findings with this test may be attributable to restriction of range of intelligence in highly selected populations. Further investigation may disclose sex differences in the predictability of this test.

Consequences Test

The Christensen, Merrifield, and Guilford (1958) Consequences Test contains ten items, each of which requires a subject to list possible consequences of an unusual situation. For example, "What would be the result if water ran uphill?" This test yields an originality score and an ideational fluency score. A variety of other versions of consequences tests have been used.

Gough (1961, 1975), studying forty-five industrial research scientists, found that neither a total score nor an originality score from the Consequences Test was related to a creativity criterion consisting of combined peer and supervisors' ratings of creativity.

Jones (1964) combined the Consequences Test with the Rensselaer Test of Creative Thinking to form a variable he called ORIG. Using a unique procedure, Jones found that ORIG was validly related to creativity ratings by managerial personnel for eighty-eight male industrial scientists and technologists.

Mullins (1959) reported that high, low, and total scores from a Consequences Test were not related to supervisors' ratings of creativity for 131 research scientists. Easily derivable answers were counted in the low score; answers at least one step removed from the direct consequences were counted in the high score.

Shapiro (1966, 1968) studied seventy-two male scientists engaged in research in a variety of fields. He found a significant relationship between originality scores from his version of the Consequences Test and a complex measure of supervisors' ratings of the scientists' creativity.

Calvin Taylor and his co-workers (Taylor and Ellison, 1964; Taylor, Smith, Ghiselin, and Ellison, 1961), in a study of 107 physical scientists, found that both a remote-high score and a total-acceptable-responses score from the Consequences Test were unrelated to three creativity criteria: supervisors' ratings of creativity and factors titled "creativity rating by laboratory chiefs" and "originality of written work."

Walker (1955) scored the Consequences Test for originality and ideational fluency. Neither score differentiated eighteen highly creative chemists and mathematicians from twelve other chemists and mathematicians. The creatives in each field were identified by expert peers.

To summarize, in four of the six studies, there was no evidence for the validity of the Consequences Test. In one study yielding support for the test's validity, scores on a consequences test were combined with other test scores. Consequences tests must therefore be considered of dubious validity as measures of scientific creativity.

Gestalt Completion Test

A number of versions of this test have been available over the years, including the Street Gestalt Completion Test and the Closure Speed Test. These tests measure "the ability to perceive an apparently disorganized or unrelated group of parts as a meaningful whole" (Thurstone and Jeffrey, 1963, p. 1). A subject has to identify a picture from which many parts have been removed. The Closure Speed Test of Thurstone and Jeffrey (1963) has twenty-four such pictures.

Helson (1971) found no differences between approximately eighteen creative and twenty-seven comparison female mathematicians on the Street Gestalt Completion Test. Creativity ratings were made by other mathematicians.

Walker (1955) found no differences on the Street Gestalt Completion Test between a group of eighteen highly creative chemists and mathematicians and twelve other chemists and mathematicians. The creatives were identified by expert peers.

The Gestalt Completion Test has shown no promise as a measure of scientific creativity.

Gestalt Transformation Test

In the Gestalt Transformation Test, a subject must select from among five objects the one which has a part that could be adapted for some new purpose. For example, one item requires selecting the object which could be used to start a fire; the alternatives are fountain pen, onion, pocket watch, bottle top, and bowling ball.

Gough (1961), studying forty-five industrial scientists, found that a correlation between the Gestalt Transformation Test and a combined peer and supervisors' rating of creativity did not quite reach significance.

Mullins (1959) found that the Gestalt Transformation Test was not significantly related to supervisors' ratings for 131 research scientists in various fields.

In summary, no significant relationships between the Gestalt Transformation Test and creativity criteria were found in two studies.

Gottschaldt Figures Test

There have been a number of variations of this test developed over the years. Guilford's Hidden Figures Test (1967b, pp. 178–79) and Witkin's Embedded Figures Test (Witkin et al., 1962) are two examples. The Gottschaldt Figures Test requires subjects to find a small geometrical figure hidden in a larger, more complex one.

Gough (1961) found no relationship between a Gottschaldt Figures Test and a combined peer and supervisors' creativity rating for forty-five industrial scientists.

Likewise, Helson (1971) found no differences between approximately eighteen creative and twenty-seven comparison women mathematicians on the Gottschaldt Figures Test. Creativity ratings were by other mathematicians.

Walker (1955) found no differences on the Hidden Figures Test between eighteen highly creative chemists and mathematicians and twelve other chemists and mathematicians. The creatives were identified by expert peers.

Thus, the Gottschaldt Figures Test showed no relationship to creativity ratings in three studies.

Ideational Fluency Test

This test requires subjects to identify as many members as possible of a broadly defined class, such as "fluids that burn."

Jones (1964), using a unique procedure, found that the Ideational Fluency Test validly related to creativity for eighty-eight male industrial scientists and technologists. Creativity was rated by management personnel.

Shapiro (1966, 1968) studied seventy-two male scientists engaged in research in a variety of fields. He found that neither of his two tests of ideational fluency, Qualities Test–Colour and Qualities Test–Shape, was significantly related to a complex measure of supervisors' ratings of the scientists' creativity.

To summarize, one study found that a test of ideational fluency was significantly related to scientific creativity, but a second study found no relationship for either of two ideational fluency tests.

Match Problems Test

A number of Match Problems tests have been developed by J. P. Guilford and his associates. These tests require subjects mentally to manipulate match sticks arranged to form various geometrical designs composed of squares. For example, a match problems test may require a subject to "remove three matches and leave the remaining match sticks in a configuration of all squares."

Gough (1961) found no relationship between a Match-Sticks Problem Test and a creativity criterion composed of peer and supervisors' ratings of creativity for forty-five industrial research scientists.

Helson (1971), using about forty-five female mathematicians, found no difference between creatives and noncreatives on a Match Problems Test. Creativity was rated by other mathematicians. However, in an earlier publication, Helson (1961), without reporting data, stated the creatives were quicker at making reconstructions required to solve the match problems.

Calvin Taylor and his co-workers (Taylor and Ellison, 1964; Taylor, Smith, Ghiselin, and Ellison, 1961) administered a Match Problems Test to 107 physical scientists and found no significant relationships with three creativity criteria: creativity ratings by laboratory chiefs, creativity ratings by supervisors, and originality of written work.

Since three studies showed no relationships with creativity criteria, Match Problems tests do not appear promising as measures of scientific creativity.

Pertinent Questions Test

In the Pertinent Questions Test, a subject is given a problem situation. He must write four questions, the answers to which would help in arriving at a decision.

Jones (1964), using a unique procedure, found no valid relationship between the Pertinent Questions Test and creativity ratings for eighty-eight male industrial scientists and technologists. Creativity was rated by managerial personnel.

Calvin Taylor and his co-workers (Taylor and Ellison, 1964; Taylor, Smith, Ghiselin, and Ellison, 1961) in a sample of 107 physical scientists found no significant relationships between the Pertinent Questions Test and three creativity criteria: creativity ratings by laboratory chiefs, creativity ratings by supervisors, and originality of written work.

The Pertinent Questions Test thus has shown no success in measuring scientific creativity.

Social Institutions Test

This test requires a subject to suggest two improvements for each of several institutions or customs (e.g., marriage).

Mullins (1959) reported that high, low, and total scores from the Social Institutions Test were all unrelated to supervisors' ratings of creativity for 131 research scientists.

Walker (1955) found no differences on the Social Institutions Test between eighteen highly creative chemists and mathematicians and twelve other chemists and mathematicians. The creatives in each field were identified by expert peers.

These studies show no evidence that the Social Institutions Test is related to real-life scientific creativity.

Unusual Uses Test

There are many versions of Unusual Uses tests. The test is sometimes called Alternate Uses, and even Guilford's Brick Uses Test is little more than a one-item version of an Unusual Uses Test. Unusual Uses tests typically consist of four to six items (e.g., paper clip, pencil) for which the subject is asked to list as many uses as he can within some time limit. The test is usually scored either for the number of different response categories used or for the number of switches from one response category to another. Some researchers also score the test for the number, quality, or originality of responses.

Gough (1961, 1975), studying forty-five industrial scientists, found that neither the total score nor an originality score from an Unusual Uses Test correlated significantly with a creativity criterion consisting of composite peer and supervisors' ratings of creativity.

Helson (1971) found no differences between approximately eighteen creative and twenty-seven comparison women mathematicians on an Unusual Uses Test. Creativity ratings were made by other mathematicians.

Jones (1964), using a unique procedure, found no valid relationship between an Alternate Uses Test and creativity ratings for eighty-eight male industrial scientists and technologists. Ratings were made by managerial personnel.

Mullins (1959) reported that only one score of four, a low quality score from an Unusual Uses Test, was significantly related to supervisors' ratings of creativity for 131 research scientists. However, four scores from a Brick Uses Test were unrelated to the same creativity criterion.

Walker (1955) scored the Brick Uses Test for the number of uses given (fluency) and for the number of times the subject shifted from one response category to another (flexibility). Walker found that eighteen highly creative chemists and mathematicians had lower flexibility scores than a control group of twelve chemists and mathematicians. No differences were found for the fluency scores. The creatives were identified by expert peers.

Thus, there is almost no evidence that the Unusual Uses Test and its variants can measure scientific creativity.

Wechsler Adult Intelligence Scale

The Wechsler Adult Intelligence Scale (WAIS) is a widely used individual intelligence test. Ten subtests are used to compute a verbal IQ, a performance IQ, and a full-scale IQ.

Helson (1971) reported no difference between creative and comparison women mathematicians on the WAIS. Only seven creatives were tested; the number of comparison women tested is not clear. Creativity ratings were made by other mathematicians.

MacKinnon (1967) reported that samples of architects and

research scientists were divided into three subsamples, ranging from most to least creative. Samples of male and female mathematicians (see Helson, 1971, above) were each divided into control and creative groups. No significant differences on the WAIS were found within any of the samples. All of these groups are described in detail in the discussion of the Minnesota Multiphasic Personality Inventory in Appendix B.

Meer and Stein (1955) administered the Wechsler-Bellevue Intelligence Scale, an earlier version of the WAIS, to twenty-four male research chemists who held the Ph.D. degree and to thirty-nine male research chemists who did not. For the non-Ph.D.'s, supervisory rankings on creativity were significantly related to full scale and performance scale scores but not to verbal scale scores. For the Ph.D.'s, however, supervisors' rankings were not significantly related to any of the Wechsler-Bellevue scale scores.

In summary, most studies found no differences between creatives and noncreatives on the WAIS. One study found a difference only for non-Ph.D.'s. Possibly the WAIS is an effective predictor of scientific creativity only in populations that are not highly selected for conventional intelligence.

Word Association Tests

A number of Word Association tests have occasionally been used as measures of creativity. Guilford's version, entitled Quick Responses, is typical. In this test, fifty words are orally presented. After each word, the subject has five seconds to write a response before the next word is presented. Scoring is generally based on rarity of responses, with the rarer responses being given greater weights.

Gough (1961, 1976) administered his Scientific Word Association Test to forty-five industrial research scientists. He related this test to a creativity criterion composed of peer and supervisors' ratings of creativity. But, since Gough tried a number of post hoc scoring approaches to see which would best predict the criterion, his research provides little evidence relevant to the validity of the Scientific Word Association Test. Gough (1976) also related a total score from the Kent-Rosanoff Word Association Test to the same creativity criterion and found no significant relationship.

MacKinnon (1962a), in a study of 124 male architects, found

that unusualness of mental associations on a Word Association Test was significantly correlated with creativity as rated by architectural experts.

Mullins (1959), using 131 research scientists, reported a significant relationship between high-quality responses on a Word Association Test and supervisors' ratings of creativity. High-quality responses were defined in terms of "the purely subjective opinion of the author." Three other scores from the test were not related to the creativity ratings.

Calvin Taylor and his associates (Taylor and Ellison, 1964; Taylor, Smith, Ghiselin, and Ellison, 1961), using a sample of 107 physical scientists, found no significant relationships between three scores on a Word Association Test and three creativity criteria: originality of written work, creativity ratings by laboratory chiefs, and supervisors' ratings of creativity.

In Walker's (1955) word association test, subjects were asked to associate freely for one minute to each of seven words. Fluency scores were based on the number of words or word groupings; flexibility scores, on the number of words or word groupings used between shifts of response categories. Neither score differentiated between eighteen highly creative chemists and mathematicians and twelve other chemists and mathematicians. The creatives were identified by expert peers.

Some small degree of promise for the word association tests is indicated by the findings of the MacKinnon and Mullins studies. However, the negative findings in the studies by Taylor and his co-workers and by Walker make it doubtful that word association tests will prove to relate to real-life scientific creativity.

Appendix B

Criterion-related Validity of Personality, Vocational, and Miscellaneous Tests

S EVEN OF THESE TESTS, which showed at least some promise as predictors of creativity in scientific fields, are reviewed in chapter 2. The remaining tests are reviewed in this appendix. See chapter 2 for an overall discussion. Under each test, studies are reviewed alphabetically by author.

Throughout this appendix, all subscales which showed significant relationships with the creativity criteria will be noted. The remaining subscales mentioned by the researchers showed nonsignificant relationships.

TESTS REVIEWED IN THIS APPENDIX

Chapin Social Insight Test
Kuder Preference Record (Vocational)
Manifest Anxiety Scale
Mechanical Comprehension Test
Minnesota Multiphasic Personality Inventory
Motivation Analysis Test
Myers-Briggs Type Indicator
Study of Values

Chapin Social Insight Test

This test attempts to "assess the perceptiveness and accuracy with which an individual can appraise others and forecast what they might say and do" (Gough, 1968, p. 1). It includes twenty-five problems, each involving a rather complex incident of social conflict or personal strife. For each problem, the subject is required to make a diagnostic evaluation or to recommend a course of action.

Gough (1961) found that the Chapin Social Insight Test correlated positively with a criterion consisting of combined peer and supervisors' ratings of creativity in a sample of forty-five industrial research scientists.

McDermid (1965) found that the Chapin Social Insight Test was unrelated to either peer or supervisory ratings of creativity in a sample of fifty-eight male engineers and technical personnel.

Further research is needed to clarify the relationship between the Chapin Social Insight Test and creativity.

Kuder Preference Record (Vocational)

The Kuder Preference Record (Vocational) yields interest scores in ten areas: outdoor, mechanical, computational, scientific, persuasive, artistic, literary, musical, social service, and clerical.

Buel and Bachner (1961), using a sample of mostly male research personnel, compared Kuder (Vocational) scores to three creativity criteria: creativity rankings and ratings by supervisory personnel and the researchers' prorated number of patents. The number of subjects used varied from forty-two to fifty-four in the comparisons. High scores in the literary area of the Kuder (Vocational) were significantly (p < .10) related to all three creativity criteria.

Jones (1964), using a unique procedure, found no valid relationship between the subscores of the Kuder Preference Record (Vocational) and creativity ratings by management personnel for eighty-eight male industrial scientists and technologists.

Further research with the Kuder Preference Record (Vocational) is needed to clarify its relationship to creativity.

Manifest Anxiety Scale

This scale (J. Taylor, 1953) consists of fifty anxiety-related items embedded in a scale of 225 items. The items are for the most part taken from the Minnesota Multiphasic Personality Inventory.

Heinze (1962) compared seventeen creative and seventeen less creative male industrial research chemists. The groups were equated for types of research in which they were engaged, supervisory levels, ages, and the length of time they had been employed by their companies. The men's creativity was rated by their colleagues and superiors. The groups did not differ on the Manifest Anxiety Scale.

MacKinnon (1965) reported that one of two groups of comparison architects scored higher than his creative architects on the Manifest Anxiety Scale.

These two studies provide little evidence for a relationship between Manifest Anxiety Scale scores and creativity.

Mechanical Comprehension Test

The Bennett Mechanical Comprehension Test is designed to measure the ability to understand a variety of mechanical elements and physical forces in practical situations. For example, a picture is presented showing several interlocking gears of various sizes, and the subject is asked to indicate the gear that will make the most turns in a minute.

Helson (1971) tested about forty-five (exact number unclear) female mathematicians and found that creative and comparison groups did not differ significantly on the Bennett Mechanical Comprehension Test. Creativity was rated by other mathematicians.

Moffie and Goodner (1968) obtained supervisors' ratings and rankings of creativity, a self-ranking of creativity, and a combined creativity product index (e.g., patents) for seventy-six males originally educated as chemical engineers. At the time of collection of the creativity data, however, the majority were in management positions. Moffie and Goodner correlated these criteria with scores on the Bennett Test of Mechanical Comprehension, administered fifteen to twenty years earlier when the men were still in college. No significant relationships were found.

Donald Taylor (1963) tested 103 male electronics personnel with the Owens-Bennett Mechanical Comprehension Test. Supervisors' ratings of creativity were significantly related to the test scores.

One of three studies showed a significant relationship between the Mechanical Comprehension Test and creativity. The relationship may be different for men and women, but with only three studies, it is impossible to tell. It would be reasonable to expect sex differences.

Minnesota Multiphasic Personality Inventory

The Minnesota Multiphasic Personality Inventory (MMPI) is a 566-item test designed to identify persons with tendencies toward certain types of psychopathology. The inventory is usually scored on fourteen scales: lie, question, validity, test-taking attitude, hypochondriasis, depression, hysteria, psychopathic deviate, masculinity-femininity, paranoia, psychasthenia, schizophrenia, hypomania, and social introversion. From time to time, researchers have created additional scales.

Gough (1961) used the MMPI with forty-five male industrial research scientists. A combination of peer and supervisors' ratings of creativity was used as the creativity criterion. Gough reported that the hypochondriasis and psychasthenia scales were significantly negatively correlated with the creativity ratings.

Heinze (1962) compared seventeen creative and seventeen less creative male industrial research chemists. Creativity was rated by the men's colleagues and superiors. The groups were equated for types of research in which they were engaged, supervisory levels, ages, and length of time they had been employed by their companies. The more creative chemists showed higher scores on Barron's ego strength scale of the MMPI. The standard MMPI scales were not administered.

Helson (1971), using about forty-five female mathematicians, found that creative women had significantly lower scores than comparison women on the hypomania scale. Creatives had higher scores on the following scales: validity, hypochondriasis, depression, psychasthenia, schizophrenia, and social introversion. The creatives also scored higher on a repression scale developed by Welsh. Creative and comparison groups were established on the basis of ratings by other mathematicians.

In a similar study (Helson and Crutchfield, 1970), the MMPI was used with male mathematicians. As in the previous study, creative and comparison groups were established on the basis of ratings by other mathematicians. There were twenty-seven to thirty-four creative and twenty-nine comparison mathematicians. The only significant finding was that creative subjects scored higher on the hypochondriasis scale.

MacKinnon and Hall (Hall and MacKinnon, 1969; MacKinnon, 1962a), using 124 male architects, reported that creativity as rated by architectural experts showed significant positive correlations with the femininity, validity (F), psychopathic deviate, and schizophrenia scales of the MMPI.

For the same sample of architects, MacKinnon (1963) reported that his creative group showed significantly higher scores on an ego strength scale of the MMPI than did one of two comparison groups of architects.

There is insufficient coherence in the results of these five studies, four of which are from the Berkeley group. Further research with the validity, schizophrenia, and ego strength scales is needed: All three scales showed positive relationships with creativity criteria in two studies.

Motivation Analysis Test

The Motivation Analysis Test measures a person's interests, drives, sentiments, and values. The 208 items of the test yield scores on five basic drives (mating, assertiveness, fear, narcism-comfort, and pugnacity-sadism) and on five sentiments (self-concept, superego, career, sweetheart-spouse, and home-parental). A variety of other scores are sometimes calculated.

Drevdahl (1961, 1964) asked 228 eminent American psychologists (plus twelve additional psychologists) to rate each other for creativity; about 80 percent of them completed the ratings. On the basis of these ratings, Drevdahl formed four groups: (1) a creative group consisting of eighteen highly rated psychologists; (2) a noncreative, nonproductive group, consisting of seven psychologists who were rated as having potential for creativity but who had shown as yet no tendency toward creative effort; (3) a noncreative, productive group, consisting of five productive psychologists of average creativity; and (4) a combined control group, consisting of the twelve psychologists in groups 2 and 3.

On the Motivation Analysis Test, Drevdahl compared the following groups: creative (1); noncreative productive (3); and combined control (4). It should be noted that group 3 is included within group 4. The only significant finding reported is that the creative psychologists showed a significantly greater attachment to home and family than did the noncreative, productive group.

Taylor, Smith, Ghiselin, and Ellison (1961) administered the Motivation Analysis Test to 107 physical scientists. Findings for only the five basic drives and five sentiments were reported. Three creativity criteria were used. The first, a factor designated as originality of written work, showed a significant positive relationship with sadism. The second criterion, creativity ratings by laboratory chiefs, showed a significant positive relationship with narcism and a significant negative relationship with assertiveness. There were no significant relationships between the Motivation Analysis scores and the third creativity criterion, supervisors' ratings of creativity.

On the basis of the inconsistent results from these two studies, there is no reason to believe that the Motivation Analysis Test will relate to scientific creativity.

Myers-Briggs Type Indicator

The Myers-Briggs Type Indicator is a forced-choice, 166-item inventory based upon Jung's theory of types. The inventory yields scores on four dimensions: extraversion vs. introversion, sensation vs. intuition, thinking vs. feeling, and judgment vs. perception. Data from these scales are sometimes reported as eight separate scores.

The Myers-Briggs test was administered by Gough (1961) to forty-five male industrial research scientists. Twelve different subscores, including some atypical ones, were not significantly correlated with a combined peer and supervisory creativity rating.

Helson (1971), using a sample of about forty-five women mathematicians, found no significant differences between a creative and a comparison group on any of the scales of the Myers-Briggs. The groups were established on the basis of creativity ratings by other mathematicians.

MacKinnon (1964) used the Myers-Briggs with 124 male architects rated for creativity by architectural editors and professors. The originality ratings correlated positively with the intuition and perception scales and negatively with the sensation and judgment scales.

Taylor and Ellison (1964) administered the Myers-Briggs to an unstated number of NASA research scientists. The authors' creativity criterion was significantly correlated only with scores on the sensation vs. intuition scale. The more creative scientists tended to be more intuitive. It is not clear whether a creativity checklist or a creativity rating scale was the criterion used.

The only consistency in the results for the Myers-Briggs Type Indicator is that the intuition scale has sometimes been positively related to creativity criteria, and the sensation scale, negatively related. However, two studies found no relationships between creativity criteria and any of the Myers-Briggs scales.

Study of Values

The Study of Values yields a profile of a subject's relative interests in six areas: theoretical, economic, aesthetic, social, political, and religious.

Buel and Bachner (1961) correlated the six scales of the Study of Values with three creativity criteria: supervisors' rankings for creativity, supervisors' ratings of creativity, and the subjects' prorated number of patents. The sample, consisting of mostly male research personnel, varied from forty-two to fifty-four in number. None of the eighteen correlations was significant.

Similarly, Gough (1961), using a sample of forty-five industrial research scientists, found that no scales from the Study of Values correlated significantly with a criterion consisting of combined peer and supervisors' ratings of creativity.

Heinze (1962) compared seventeen creative and seventeen less creative male industrial research chemists. Creativity was rated by colleagues and superiors. The groups were equated for types of research in which they were engaged, supervisory levels, age, and the length of time they had been employed by their companies. The more creative chemists held significantly higher economic and aesthetic values and significantly lower religious values than the less creative chemists.

The Study of Values was used by Helson and Crutchfield

(1970) in a study of twenty-seven to thirty-four creative and twenty-nine comparison male mathematicians. These groups were established on the basis of creativity ratings by experts in mathematics. The creative group scored significantly lower on the religion scale of the Study of Values.

MacKinnon (1962b), studying 124 architects rated for creativity by architectural experts, found that a group of creative architects was significantly lower than two comparison groups of architects on the economic scale of the Study of Values. Creativity ratings showed significant positive correlations with theoretical and aesthetic values and a significant negative correlation with economic values in the sample of 124 architects.

There are few common threads in the findings of these six studies which used the Study of Values. The religion scale showed a negative relationship to creativity in two studies, and the aesthetic scale showed a positive relationship in two studies.

References

AC Spark Plug Division, General Motors Corporation. *AC Test of Creative Ability: Test administration manual.* Chicago: Industrial Relations Center, University of Chicago, 1959.

Albright, L. E., and Glennon, J. R. Personal history correlates of physical scientists' career aspirations. *Journal of Applied Psychology,* 1961, *45,* 281–84.

Allison, P. D., and Stewart, J. A. Productivity differences among scientists: Evidence for accumulative advantage. *American Sociological Review,* 1974, *39,* 596–606.

American Institute for Research. *A Test for Selecting Research Personnel.* Pittsburgh: American Institute for Research, 1954.

Anastasi, A. *Psychological testing,* 4th ed. New York: Macmillan, 1976.

Arieti, S. *Creativity: The magic synthesis.* New York: Basic Books, 1976.

Austin, J. H. *Chase, chance, and creativity.* New York: Columbia University Press, 1978.

Ausubel, D. P. Fostering creativity in the school. In D. W. Brison (ed.), *Accelerated learning and fostering creativity.* Toronto: Ontario Institute for Studies in Education, 1968. Pp. 10–16.

Barber, B., and Fox, R. C. The case of the floppy-eared rabbits: An instance of serendipity gained and serendipity lost. In B. Barber and W. Hirsch (eds.), *The sociology of science.* New York: Free Press, 1962. Pp. 525–38.

Barron, F. Creative vision and expression in writing and painting. In *The creative person,* proceedings of a conference presented at the University of California Alumni Center, Lake Tahoe, California, 1961.

Barron, F. The disposition toward originality. In C. W. Taylor and F. Barron (eds.), *Scientific creativity.* New York: Wiley, 1963.

Barron, F. The psychology of the creative writer. *Theory into Practice,* 1966, *5,* 157–59.

Barron, F. *Creativity and personal freedom.* Princeton: Van Nostrand, 1968.

Barron, F. *Creative person and creative process.* New York: Holt, Rinehart and Winston, 1969.

Barron, F., and Welsh, G. S. Artistic perception as a possible factor in personality style: Its measurement by a figure preference test. *Journal of Psychology,* 1952, *33,* 199–203.

Bartlett, M. M., and Davis, G. A. Do the Wallach and Kogan tests predict real creative behavior? *Perceptual and Motor Skills,* 1974, *39,* 730.

Bayer, A. E., and Folger, J. Some correlates of a citation measure of productivity in science. *Sociology of Education,* 1966, *39,* 381–90.

Bennett, G. K. Factors affecting the value of validation studies. *Personnel Psychology,* 1969, *22,* 265–68.

Bergum, B. O. Self-perceptions of creativity among academic inventors and non-inventors. *Perceptual and Motor Skills,* 1975, *40,* 78.

Birns, B. Individual differences in human neonates' responses to stimulation. *Child Development,* 1965, *36,* 249–56.

Blade, E. Creative science. In M. A. Coler (ed.), *Essays on creativity in the sciences.* New York: New York University Press, 1963. Pp. 183–206.

Blume, S. S., and Sinclair, R. Chemists in British universities: A study of the reward system in science. *American Sociological Review,* 1973, *38,* 126–38.

Brogden, H. E., and Sprecher, T. B. Criteria of creativity. In

C. W. Taylor (ed.), *Creativity: Progress and potential.* New York: McGraw-Hill, 1964. Pp. 155–76.

Brooks, J. B. The behavioral significance of childhood experiences that are reported in life history interviews. Doctoral dissertation, University of California, Berkeley, 1963. *Dissertation Abstracts,* 1963, *24,* 1242–43. (University Microfilms No. 63-5488.)

Brown, J. L. States in newborn infants. *Merrill-Palmer Quarterly,* 1964, *10,* 313–27.

Buel, W. D. Biographical data and the identification of creative research personnel. *Journal of Applied Psychology,* 1965, *49,* 318–21.

Buel, W. D., and Bachner, V. M. The assessment of creativity in a research setting. *Journal of Applied Psychology,* 1961, *45,* 353–58.

Burns, R. K.; Harris, R. H.; and Hendrix, A. A. Research on measuring creative ability of engineers, foremen and other management personnel in General Motors: A research report. General Motors, July 12, 1957.

Buros, O. K., ed. *The fifth mental measurements yearbook.* Highland Park, N. J.: Gryphon Press, 1959.

Buros, O. K., ed. *The sixth mental measurements yearbook.* Highland Park, N. J.: Gryphon Press, 1965.

Buros, O. K., ed. *The seventh mental measurements yearbook.* Vols. I and II. Highland Park, N. J.: Gryphon Press, 1972.

Buros, O. K., ed. *The eighth mental measurements yearbook.* Vols. I and II. Highland Park, N. J.: Gryphon Press, 1978.

Burton, R. V. Validity of retrospective reports assessed by the multitrait-multimethod analysis. *Developmental Psychology Monograph,* 1970, *3* (3, Part 2).

Busse, T. V. Childrearing correlates of flexible thinking. Unpublished doctoral dissertation, University of Chicago, 1967.

Busse, T. V. Child-rearing antecedents of flexible thinking. *Developmental Psychology,* 1969, *1,* 585–91.

Busse, T. V., and Busse, P. Negro parental behavior and social class variables. *Journal of Genetic Psychology,* 1972, *120,* 287–94.

Busse, T. V., and Mansfield, R. S. Theories of the creative process: A review and a perspective. *Journal of Creative Behavior,* 1980, *14,* 91–103 ff.

Campbell, D. P. *Strong Vocational Interest Blanks: Manual, 1969 supplement.* Stanford, California: Stanford University Press, 1969.

Cannon, W. B. *The way of an investigator.* New York: Norton, 1945.

Chambers, J. A. Relating personality and biographical factors to scientific creativity. *Psychological Monographs,* 1964, *78* (7, Whole No. 584).

Chambers, J. A. Beginning a multidimensional theory of creativity. *Psychological Reports,* 1969, *25,* 779–99.

Chambers, J. A. College teachers: Their effect on creativity of students. *Journal of Educational Psychology,* 1973, *65,* 326–34.

Chandrasekhar, S. Shakespeare, Newton, and Beethoven or patterns of creativity. Chicago: University of Chicago Center for Policy Study, 1975.

Christensen, P. R.; Merrifield, P. R.; and Guilford, J. P. *Consequences Test.* Beverly Hills, Ca.: Sheridan Supply Company, 1958.

Christie, T. Environmental factors in creativity. *Journal of Creative Behavior,* 1970, *4,* 13–31.

Clark, K. E. *America's psychologists: A survey of a growing profession.* Washington, D. C.: American Psychological Association, 1957.

Clifford, P. I. Emotional contacts with the external world manifested by a selected group of highly creative chemists and mathematicians. *Perceptual and Motor Skills,* 1958, *8,* 3–26.

Cline, V. B.; Tucker, M. F.; and Anderson, D. R. Psychology of the scientist: XX. Cross-validation of biographical information predictor keys across diverse samples of scientists. *Psychological Reports,* 1966, *19,* 951–54.

Cole, J. R., and Cole, S. Measuring the quality of sociological research: Problems in the use of the *Science Citation Index. American Sociologist,* 1971, *6,* 23–29.

Cole, J. R., and Cole, S. The Ortega hypothesis. *Science,* 1972, *178,* 368–75.

Cole, J. R., and Cole, S. *Social stratification in science.* Chicago: University of Chicago Press, 1973.

Cole, S. Professional standing and the reception of scientific discoveries. *American Journal of Sociology,* 1970, *76,* 286–306.

Cole, S., and Cole, J. R. Scientific output and recognition: A study in the operation of the reward system in science. *American Sociological Review,* 1967, *32,* 377–90.

Crockenberg, S. B. Creativity tests: A boon or boondoggle for education? *Review of Educational Research,* 1972, *42,* 27–45.

Cronbach, L. J. Test validation. In R. L. Thorndike (ed.), *Educational measurement,* 2d ed. Washington: American Council on Education, 1971. Pp. 443–507.

Cronbach, L. J., and Meehl, P. E. Construct validity in psychological tests. *Psychological Bulletin,* 1955, *52,* 281–302.

Cross, P. G.; Cattell, R. B.; and Butcher, H. J. The personality patterns of creative artists. *British Journal of Educational Psychology,* 1967, *37,* 292–99.

Curie, E. *Madame Curie.* Translated by V. Sheean. Garden City, N. Y.: Garden City Publishing Co., 1937.

Datta, L. A note on the Remote Associates Test, United States culture, and creativity. *Journal of Applied Psychology,* 1964, *48,* 184–85. (a)

Datta, L. Remote Associates Test as a predictor of creativity in engineers. *Journal of Applied Psychology,* 1964, *48,* 183. (b)

Datta, L. Birth order and early scientific attainment. *Perceptual and Motor Skills,* 1967, *24,* 157–58. (a)

Datta, L. Family religious background and early scientific creativity. *American Sociological Review,* 1967, *32,* 626–35. (b)

Datta, L. Birth order and potential scientific creativity. *Sociometry,* 1968, *31,* 76–88.

Datta, L., and Parloff, M. B. On the relevance of autonomy: parent-child relationships and early scientific creativity. *Proceedings, 75th Annual Convention of the American Psychological Association,* 1967, *2,* 149–50.

Davis, G. A. Instruments useful in studying creative behavior and creative talent: Part II, noncommercially available instruments. *Journal of Creative Behavior,* 1971, *5,* 162–65.

Dellas, M., and Gaier, E. L. Identification of creativity: The individual. *Psychological Bulletin,* 1970, *73,* 55–73.

Dennis, W. The bibliographies of eminent scientists. *Scientific Monthly,* 1954, *79,* 180–83.

Denny, D. A. Identification of teacher-classroom variables facilitating pupil creative growth. *American Educational Research Journal,* 1968, *5,* 365–83.

Drevdahl, J. E. A study of the etiology and development of the creative personality. Coral Gables, Florida: Miami University, 1961. (ERIC Document Reproduction Service No. ED 002 776.)

Drevdahl, J. E. Some developmental and environmental factors in creativity. In C. W. Taylor (ed.), *Widening horizons in creativity*. New York: Wiley, 1964. Pp. 170–86.

Drevdahl, J. E., and Cattell, R. B. Personality and creativity in artists and writers. *Journal of Clinical Psychology*, 1958, *14*, 107–11.

Edge, D. O., and Mulkay, M. J. *Astronomy transformed: The emergence of radio astronomy in Britain*. New York: Wiley, 1976.

Eisenstadt, J. M. Parental loss and genius. *American Psychologist*, 1978, *33*, 211–23.

Ellison, R. L. The relationship of certain biographical information to success in science. Unpublished master's thesis, University of Utah, 1960.

Ellison, R. L.; James, L. R.; and Carron, T. J. Prediction of R & D performance criteria with biographical information. *Journal of Industrial Psychology*, 1970, *5*, 37–57.

Feldhusen, J. F.; Treffinger, D. J.; and Bahlke, S. J. Developing creative thinking: The Purdue creativity program. *Journal of Creative Behavior*, 1970, *4*, 85–90.

Feldman, D. The developmental approach: Universal to unique. In S. Rosner and L. E. Abt (eds.), *Essays in creativity*. Croton-on-Hudson, N. Y.: North River Press, 1974. Pp. 47–85.

French, J. W.; Ekstrom, R. B.; and Price, L. A. *Manual for kit of reference tests for cognitive factors* (Revised edition). Princeton, N. J.: Educational Testing Service, 1963.

Getzels, J. W. Creativity: Prospects and issues. In I. A. Taylor and J. W. Getzels (eds.), *Perspectives in creativity*. Chicago: Aldine, 1975. Pp. 326–44.

Getzels, J. W., and Csikszentmihalyi, M. From problem solving to problem finding. In I. A. Taylor and J. W. Getzels (eds.), *Perspectives in creativity*. Chicago: Aldine, 1975. Pp. 90–116.

Getzels, J. W., and Csikszentmihalyi, M. *The creative vision*. New York: Wiley, 1976.

Ghiselin, B. *The creative process*. Berkeley: University of California Press, 1952.

Ghiselli, E. E. The forced-choice technique in self-description. *Personnel Psychology,* 1954, *7,* 201–8.

Ghiselli, E. E. A scale for the measurement of initiative. *Personnel Psychology,* 1955, *8,* 157–64.

Goodman, P.; Furcon, J.; and Rose, J. Examination of some measures of creative ability by the multitrait-multimethod matrix. *Journal of Applied Psychology,* 1969, *53,* 240–43.

Gordon, G. The identification and use of creative abilities in scientific organizations. In C. W. Taylor (ed.), *Climate for creativity.* New York: Pergamon Press, 1972. Pp. 109–24.

Gough, H. G. Techniques for identifying the creative research scientist. In *The creative person,* proceedings of a conference presented at the University of California Alumni Center, Lake Tahoe, Ca., 1961.

Gough, H. G. *The Chapin Social Insight Test: Manual.* Palo Alto, Ca.: Consulting Psychologists Press, 1968.

Gough, H. G. A new Scientific Uses Test and its relationship to creativity in research. *Journal of Creative Behavior,* 1975, *9,* 245–52.

Gough, H. G. Studying creativity by means of word association tests. *Journal of Applied Psychology,* 1976, *61,* 348–53.

Gough, H. G., and Heilbrun, A. B. *The Adjective Check List: Manual.* Palo Alto, Ca.: Consulting Psychologists Press, 1965.

Gruber, H. E. *Darwin on man: A psychological study of scientific creativity,* together with Darwin's early and unpublished notebooks transcribed and annotated by P. H. Barrett. New York: Dutton, 1974.

Guilford, J. P. Intellectual resources and their values as seen by scientists. In C. W. Taylor and F. Barron (eds.), *Scientific creativity.* New York: Wiley, 1963. Pp. 101–18.

Guilford, J. P. Creativity: Yesterday, today, and tomorrow. *Journal of Creative Behavior,* 1967, *1,* 3–14. (a)

Guilford, J. P. *The nature of human intelligence.* New York: McGraw-Hill, 1967. (b)

Guilford, J. P. Some misconceptions regarding measurement of creative talents. *Journal of Creative Behavior,* 1971, *5,* 77–87.

Guilford, J. P., and Hoepfner, R. *The analysis of intelligence.* New York: McGraw-Hill, 1971.

Hadamard, J. *The psychology of invention in the mathematical field.* Princeton: Princeton University Press, 1945.

Hall, W. B. A technique for assessing aesthetic predispositions: Mosaic Construction Test. *Journal of Creative Behavior,* 1972, *6,* 225–35.

Hall, W. B., and MacKinnon, D. W. Personality inventory correlates of creativity among architects. *Journal of Applied Psychology,* 1969, *53,* 322–26.

Harmon, L. R. The development of a criterion of scientific competence. In C. W. Taylor and F. Barron (eds.), *Scientific creativity.* New York: Wiley, 1963. Pp. 44–52.

Harris, R. H. The development and validation of a test of creative ability. Doctoral dissertation, Purdue University, 1955. *Dissertation Abstracts,* 1955, *15,* 1891. (University Microfilms No. 55–624.)

Haslerud, G. M. *Transfer, memory, & creativity.* Minneapolis: University of Minnesota Press, 1972.

Heinze, S. J. Job adaptation and creativity in industrial research scientists. Doctoral dissertation, University of Chicago, 1962.

Helson, R. Creativity, sex, and mathematics. In *The creative person,* proceedings of a conference presented at the University of California Alumni Center, Lake Tahoe, Ca., 1961.

Helson, R. Sex differences in creative style. *Journal of Personality,* 1967, *35,* 214–33.

Helson, R. Women mathematicians and the creative personality. *Journal of Consulting and Clinical Psychology,* 1971, *36,* 210–20.

Helson, R., and Crutchfield, R. S. Mathematicians: The creative researcher and the average Ph.D. *Journal of Consulting and Clinical Psychology,* 1970, *34,* 250–57.

Holland, J. L. Creative and academic performance among talented adolescents. *Journal of Educational Psychology,* 1961, *52,* 136–47.

Hudson, L. *Contrary imaginations.* London: Methuen and Company, 1966.

Jackson, P. W., and Messick, S. The person, the product, and the response: Conceptual problems in the assessment of creativity. In J. Kagan (ed.), *Creativity and learning.* Boston: Houghton Mifflin, 1967. Pp. 1–19.

Jones, F. E. Predictor variables for creativity in industrial science. *Journal of Applied Psychology,* 1964, *48,* 134–36.

Kaltsounis, B. Instruments useful in studying creative behavior and creative talent: Part I, commercially available instruments. *Journal of Creative Behavior,* 1971, *5,* 117–26.

Kaltsounis, B. Additional instruments useful in studying creative behavior and creative talent: Part III, non-commercially available instruments. *Journal of Creative Behavior,* 1972, *6,* 268–74.

Keating, D. P., ed. *Intellectual talent: Research and development.* Baltimore: Johns Hopkins University Press, 1976.

Koestler, A. *The act of creation.* New York: Macmillan, 1964.

Kogan, N., and Pankove, E. Creative ability over a five-year span. *Child Development,* 1972, *43,* 427–42.

Kogan, N., and Pankove, E. Long-term predictive validity of divergent-thinking tests: Some negative evidence. *Journal of Educational Psychology,* 1974, *66,* 802–10.

Köhler, W. *The task of gestalt psychology.* Princeton: Princeton University Press, 1969.

Kris, E. *Psychoanalytic explorations in art.* New York: International Universities Press, 1952.

Kubie, L. S. *Neurotic distortion of the creative process.* New York: Noonday Press, 1958.

Kuhn, T. S. *The structure of scientific revolutions,* 2d ed. Chicago: University of Chicago Press, 1970.

Lehman, H. C., and Witty, P. A. Scientific eminence and church membership. *Scientific Monthly,* 1931, *33,* 544–49.

Lent, R. H.; Aurbach, H. A.; and Levin, L. S. Predictors, criteria, and significant results. *Personnel Psychology,* 1971, *24,* 519–33.

Libby, W. F. Creativity in science. In J. D. Roslansky (ed.), *Creativity: A discussion at the Nobel Conference.* Amsterdam: North Holland Publishing Company, 1970. Pp. 33–52.

Lindsey, D. Distinction, achievement, and editorial board membership. *American Psychologist,* 1976, *31,* 799–804.

Loewi, O. *From the workshop of discoveries.* Lawrence, Kan.: University of Kansas Press, 1953.

Lynn, D. B. *The father: His role in child development.* Monterey, Ca.: Brooks/Cole, 1974.

MacCurdy, R. D. Characteristics and backgrounds of superior science students. *School Review,* 1956, *64,* 67–71.

MacKinnon, D. W. Creativity in architects. In *The creative person,* proceedings of a conference presented at the University of California Alumni Center, Lake Tahoe, Ca., 1961.

MacKinnon, D. W. The nature and nurture of creative talent. *American Psychologist,* 1962, *17,* 484–95. (a)

MacKinnon, D. W. The personality correlates of creativity: A study of American architects. In S. Coopersmith (ed.), *Proceedings of the XIV International Congress of Applied Psychology, Volume II: Personality research.* Copenhagen: Munksgaard, 1962. Pp. 11–39. (b)

MacKinnon, D. W. Creativity and images of the self. In R. W. White (ed.), *The study of lives.* New York: Atherton, 1963. Pp. 250–78.

MacKinnon, D. W. The creativity of architects. In C. W. Taylor (ed.), *Widening horizons in creativity.* New York: Wiley, 1964. Pp. 359–78.

MacKinnon, D. W. Personality and the realization of creative potential. *American Psychologist,* 1965, *20,* 273–81.

MacKinnon, D. W. Educating for creativity: A modern myth? In P. Heist (ed.), *Educating for creativity: A modern myth?* Berkeley, Ca.: Center for Research and Development in Higher Education, 1967. Pp. 1–20.

MacKinnon, D. W. Childhood variables and adult personality in two professional samples: Architects and research scientists. In F. E. Williams (ed.), *Creativity at home and in school.* St. Paul, Minn.: Macalester College, 1968. Pp. 124–60. (a)

MacKinnon, D. W. Selecting students with creative potential. In P. Heist (ed.), *The creative college student: An unmet challenge.* San Francisco: Jossey-Bass, 1968. Pp. 101–16. (b)

Maddi, S. R. Motivational aspects of creativity. *Journal of Personality,* 1965, *33,* 330–47.

Maddi, S. R. The strenuousness of the creative life. In I. A. Taylor and J. W. Getzels (eds.), *Perspectives in creativity.* Chicago: Aldine, 1975. Pp. 173–90.

Mansfield, R. S., and Busse, T. V. The effectiveness of creativity training programs. *Childhood Education,* 1974, *51,* 53–56.

Mansfield, R. S.; Busse, T. V.; and Krepelka, E. J. The effectiveness of creativity training. *Review of Educational Research,* 1978, *48,* 517–36.

Maslow, A. H. Creativity in self-actualizing people. In H. H. Anderson (ed.), *Creativity and its cultivation.* New York: Harper and Row, 1959. Pp. 83–95.

Maslow, A. H. The creative attitude. In R. L. Mooney and T. A. Razik (eds.), *Explorations in creativity*. New York: Harper and Row, 1967. Pp. 43–54.

May, R. *The courage to create*. New York: Norton, 1975.

McDermid, C. D. Some correlates of creativity in engineering personnel. *Journal of Applied Psychology*, 1965, *49*, 14–19.

Mednick, S. A. The associative basis of the creative process. *Psychological Review*, 1962, *69*, 220–32.

Mednick, S. A., and Mednick, M. T. *Remote Associates Test: Examiner's Manual*. Boston: Houghton Mifflin, 1967.

Meehl, P. E. The creative individual: Why it is hard to identify him. In G. A. Steiner (ed.), *The creative organization*. Chicago: University of Chicago Press, 1965. Pp. 25–34.

Meer, B., and Stein, M. I. Measures of intelligence and creativity. *Journal of Psychology*, 1955, *39*, 117–26.

Meltzer, B. N. The productivity of social scientists. *American Journal of Sociology*, 1949, *55*, 25–29.

Mendelsohn, G. A. Associative and attentional processes in creative performance. *Journal of Personality*, 1976, *44*, 341–69.

Merton, R. K. *Social theory and social structure,* enlarged ed. New York: Free Press, 1968.

Merton, R. K. *The sociology of science*. Edited and with an introduction by N. W. Storer. Chicago: University of Chicago Press, 1973.

Moffie, D. J., and Goodner, S. *A predictive validity study of creative and effective managerial performance*. Greensboro, N.C.: The Creativity Research Institute of Smith Richardson Foundation, 1968.

Montour, K. William James Sidis, The broken twig. *American Psychologist*, 1977, *32*, 265–79.

Morrison, R. F. Factored life history antecedents of industrial research performance. Doctoral dissertation, Purdue University, 1961. *Dissertation Abstracts*, 1962, *22*, 2459. (University Microfilms No. 61-6552.)

Moulin, L. The Nobel prizes for the sciences from 1901–1950—An essay in sociological analysis. *British Journal of Sociology*, 1955, *6*, 246–63.

Mullins, C. J. Prediction of creativity in a sample of research scientists. WADC-TN-59-36. ASTIA Document No. AD 211 039. Lackland Air Force Base, Tex.: Personnel Laboratory, Wright Air Development Center, 1959.

Myden, W. Interpretation and evaluation of certain personality characteristics involved in creative production. *Perceptual and Motor Skills,* 1959, *9,* 139–58.

Nicholls, J. G. Creativity in the person who will never produce anything original and useful: The concept of creativity as a normally distributed trait. *American Psychologist,* 1972, *27,* 717–27.

Nichols, R. C. Parental attitudes of mothers of intelligent adolescents and creativity of their children. *Child Development,* 1964, *35,* 1041–49.

Nichols, R. C., and Holland, J. L. Prediction of the first year college performance of high aptitude students. *Psychological Monographs,* 1963, *77* (7, Whole No. 570).

Olby, R. *The path to the double helix.* Seattle: University of Washington Press, 1974.

Owens, W. Cognitive, noncognitive, and environmental correlates of mechanical ingenuity. *Journal of Applied Psychology,* 1969, *53,* 199–208.

Parloff, M. B.; Datta, L.; Kleman, M.; and Handlon, J. H. Personality characteristics which differentiate creative male adolescents and adults. *Journal of Personality,* 1968, *36,* 528–52.

Parnes, S. J.; Noller, R. B.; and Biondi, A. M. *Guide to creative action.* New York: Scribner's, 1977.

Pelz, D. C., and Andrews, F. M. *Scientists in organizations,* rev. ed. Ann Arbor: Institute for Social Research, University of Michigan, 1976.

Raychaudhuri, M. Relation of creativity and sex to Rorschach M responses. *Journal of Personality Assessment,* 1971, *35,* 27–31.

Reskin, B. F. Scientific productivity and the reward structure of science. *American Sociological Review,* 1977, *42,* 491–504.

Robbins, L. C. The accuracy of parental recall of aspects of child development and of child rearing practices. *Journal of Abnormal and Social Psychology,* 1963, *66,* 261–70.

Roe, A. A psychological study of eminent biologists. *Psychological Monographs,* 1951, *65* (14, Whole No. 331). (a)

Roe, A. A psychological study of physical scientists. *Genetic Psychology Monographs,* 1951, *43,* 121–235. (b)

Roe, A. *The making of a scientist.* New York: Dodd, Mead, 1952.

Roe, A. A psychological study of eminent psychologists and

anthropologists, and a comparison with biological and physical scientists. *Psychological Monographs,* 1953, *67* (2, Whole No. 352).

Roe, A. Changes in scientific activities with age. *Science,* 1965, *150,* 313–18.

Rogers, C. R. Toward a theory of creativity. In H. H. Anderson (ed.), *Creativity and its cultivation.* New York: Harper and Row, 1959. Pp. 69–82.

Rogers, C. R. *Freedom to learn.* Columbus: Merrill, 1969.

Rokeach, M. In pursuit of the creative process. In G. A. Steiner (ed.), *The creative organization.* Chicago: University of Chicago Press, 1965. Pp. 66–105.

Rosner, S., and Abt, L. E., eds. *The creative experience.* New York: Dell, 1972.

Rossman, B. B., and Gollob, H. F. Comparison of social judgments of creativity and intelligence. *Journal of Personality and Social Psychology,* 1975, *31,* 271–81.

Schachtel, E. G. *Metamorphosis.* New York: Basic Books, 1959.

Schachter, S. Birth order, eminence and higher education. *American Sociological Review,* 1963, *28,* 757–68.

Schaefer, C. E., and Anastasi, A. A biographical inventory for identifying creativity in adolescent boys. *Journal of Applied Psychology,* 1968, *52,* 42–48.

Schmidt, F. L.; Hunter, J. E.; and Urry, V. W. Statistical power in criterion-related validation studies. *Journal of Applied Psychology,* 1976, *61,* 473–85.

Segal, S.; Busse, T. V.; and Mansfield, R. S. The relationship of scientific creativity in the biological sciences to predoctoral accomplishments and experiences. *American Educational Research Journal,* in press.

Shapiro, R. J. The identification of creative research scientists. *Psychologia Africana,* 1966, *11,* 99–132.

Shapiro, R. J. Creative research scientists. *Psychologia Africana Monograph Supplement* No. 4, 1968.

Shockley, W. On the statistics of individual variations of productivity in research laboratories. *Proceedings of the Institute of Radio Engineers,* 1957, *45,* 279–90.

Skinner, B. F. A case history in scientific method. In S. Koch (ed.), *Psychology: A study of a science.* Vol. 2. New York: McGraw-Hill, 1959. Pp. 359–79.

Smith, W. J.; Albright, L. E.; Glennon, J. R.; and Owens, W. A. The prediction of research competence and creativity from personal history. *Journal of Applied Psychology*, 1961, *45*, 59–62.

Sprecher, T. B. An investigation of criteria for creativity in engineers. Doctoral dissertation, University of Maryland, 1957. *Dissertation Abstracts*, 1958, *18*, 1101–2. (University Microfilms No. 58-4733.)

Sprecher, T. B. A study of engineers' criteria for creativity. *Journal of Applied Psychology*, 1959, *43*, 141–48.

Stanley, J. C.; George, W. C.; and Solano, C. H., eds. *The gifted and the creative: A fifty-year perspective.* Baltimore, Md.: Johns Hopkins University Press, 1977.

Stanley, J. C.; Keating, D. P.; and Fox, L. H., eds. *Mathematical talent: Discovery, description, and development.* Baltimore, Md.: Johns Hopkins University Press, 1974.

Stanley, J. C., and Thomasson, P. Peer-rated "creativity" of prominent psychometricians. *Psychological Newsletter*, 1957, *9*, 1–6.

Stein, M. I. Creativity and the scientist. Paper presented at the National Physical Laboratory, Teddington, Middlesex, England, 1956.

Stein, M. I. Creativity and the scientist. In B. Barber and W. Hirsch (eds.), *The sociology of science.* New York: Free Press, 1962. Pp. 329–43.

Stein, M. I. A transactional approach to creativity. In C. W. Taylor and F. Barron (eds.), *Scientific creativity.* New York: Wiley, 1963. Pp. 217–27.

Stein, M. I. *Stimulating creativity: Individual procedures.* Vol. 1. New York: Academic Press, 1974.

Stein, M. I. *Stimulating creativity: Group procedures.* Vol. 2. New York: Academic Press, 1975.

Strong, E. K., Jr. *Strong Vocational Interest Blanks: Manual.* Revised by D. P. Campbell. Stanford, Ca.: Stanford University Press, 1966.

Stuteville, J. R. The life history patterns of highly creative inventors. Doctoral dissertation, University of California, Los Angeles, 1966. *Dissertation Abstracts*, 1967, *27*, 3551A–3552A. (University Microfilms No. 67-4498.)

Taylor, C. W., and Ellison, R. L. Predicting creative performances from multiple measures. In C. W. Taylor (ed.), *Widening horizons in creativity.* New York: Wiley, 1964. Pp. 227–60.

Taylor, C. W., and Ellison, R. L. Biographical predictors of scientific performance. *Science,* 1967, *155,* 1075–80.

Taylor, C. W.; Ellison, R. L.; and Tucker, M. F. Biographical information and the prediction of multiple criteria of success in science. National Aeronautics and Space Administration, Washington. Research Project NASA-105, September, 1965. Also published by the Creativity Research Institute of the Richardson Foundation, 1966. (ERIC Document Reproduction Service No. ED 020 148.)

Taylor, C. W.; Smith, W. R.; and Ghiselin, B. Productivity and creativity of scientists at an Air Force research center. In G. Finch (ed.), *Symposium on Air Force human engineering, personnel, and training research.* Washington, D. C.: National Academy of Sciences—National Research Council, 1960. Pp. 132–43.

Taylor, C. W.; Smith, W. R.; and Ghiselin, B. The creative and other contributions of one sample of research scientists. In C. W. Taylor and F. Barron (eds.), *Scientific creativity.* New York: Wiley, 1963. Pp. 53–76.

Taylor, C. W.; Smith, W. R.; Ghiselin, B.; and Ellison, R. Explorations in the measurement and prediction of contributions of one sample of scientists. Technical report ASD-TR-61-96. Lackland Air Force Base, Tex.: Personnel Laboratory, 1961.

Taylor, D. W. Variables related to creativity and productivity among men in two research laboratories. In C. W. Taylor (ed.), *The second (1957) University of Utah research conference on the identification of creative scientific talent.* Salt Lake City: University of Utah Press, 1958. Pp. 20–54.

Taylor, D. W. Variables related to creativity and productivity among men in two research laboratories. In C. W. Taylor and F. Barron (eds.), *Scientific creativity.* New York: Wiley, 1963. Pp. 228–50.

Taylor, J. A. A personality scale of manifest anxiety. *Journal of Abnormal and Social Psychology,* 1953, *48,* 285–90.

Thomas, A., and Chess, S. *Temperament and development.* New York: Brunner/Mazel, 1977.

Thomas, A.; Chess, S.; and Birch, H. G. The origin of personality. *Scientific American,* 1970, *223,* 102–9.

Thorndike, R. L. Some methodological issues in the study of creativity. In A. Anastasi (ed.), *Testing problems in per-*

spective. Washington, D. C.: American Council on Education, 1966. Pp. 436–48.

Thurstone, L. L. Criteria of scientific success and the selection of scientific talent. In C. W. Taylor (ed.), *Widening horizons in creativity.* New York: Wiley, 1964. Pp. 10–16.

Thurstone, L. L., and Jeffrey, T. E. *Closure Speed: Test administration manual.* Chicago: Industrial Relations Center, University of Chicago, 1963.

Thurstone, T. G., and Mellinger, J. J. *CREE Questionnaire: Test administration manual.* Chicago: Industrial Relations Center, University of Chicago, 1959.

Torrance, E. P. *Guiding creative talent.* Englewood Cliffs, N. J.: Prentice Hall, 1962.

Torrance, E. P. *Rewarding creative behavior.* Englewood Cliffs, N. J.: Prentice Hall, 1965.

Torrance, E. P. *Torrance Tests of Creative Thinking: Norms-technical manual.* Princeton, N. J.: Personnel Press, 1966.

Treffinger, D. J.; Renzulli, J. S.; and Feldhusen, J. F. Problems in the assessment of creative thinking. *Journal of Creative Behavior,* 1971, *5,* 104–12.

Tucker, M. F.; Cline, V. B.; and Schmitt, J. R. Prediction of creativity and other performance measures from biographical information among pharmaceutical scientists. *Journal of Applied Psychology,* 1967, *51,* 131–38.

Ulam, S. M. *Adventures of a mathematician.* New York: Charles Scribner's Sons, 1976.

Walberg, H. J. A portrait of the artist and the scientist as young men: I. Biographical characteristics of award winners in the two cultures. United States Department of Health, Education and Welfare, Office of Education, 1967. (ERIC Document Reproduction Service No. ED 019 679.)

Walker, D. E. The relationship between creativity and selected test behaviors for chemists and mathematicians. Unpublished doctoral dissertation, University of Chicago, 1955.

Wallach, M. A. Review of Torrance Tests of Creative Thinking. *American Educational Research Journal,* 1968, *5,* 272–81.

Wallach, M. A. Creativity. In P. H. Mussen (ed.), *Carmichael's manual of child psychology.* Vol. 1, 3d ed. New York: Wiley, 1970. Pp. 1211–72.

Wallach, M. A. *The intelligence/creativity distinction.* New York: General Learning Press, 1971.

Wallach, M. A. Psychology of talent and graduate education. In S. Messick (ed.), *Individuality in learning.* San Francisco: Jossey-Bass, 1976. Pp. 178–210.

Wallach, M. A., and Kogan, N. *Modes of thinking in young children.* New York: Holt, Rinehart and Winston, 1965.

Wallach, M. A., and Wing, C. W. *The talented student.* New York: Holt, Rinehart and Winston, 1969.

Watson, J. D. *The double helix.* New York: Atheneum, 1968.

Welsh, G. S. *Creativity and intelligence: A personality approach.* Chapel Hill, N. C.: Institute for Research in Social Science, 1975.

Wertheimer, M. *Productive thinking,* enlarged ed. New York: Harper and Row, 1959.

White, M. J., and White, K. G. Citation analysis of psychology journals. *American Psychologist,* 1977, *32,* 301–5.

Wiener, N. *Ex-prodigy: My childhood and youth.* New York: Simon and Schuster, 1953.

Witkin, H. A.; Dyk, R. B.; Faterson, H. F.; Goodenough, D. R.; and Karp, S. A. *Psychological differentiation.* New York: Wiley, 1962.

Yamamoto, K. Validation of tests of creative thinking: A review of some studies. *Exceptional Children,* 1965, *31,* 281–90.

Yarrow, M. R. Problems of methods in parent-child research. *Child Development,* 1963, *34,* 215–26.

Yarrow, M. R.; Campbell, J. D.; and Burton, R. V. Recollections of childhood: A study of the retrospective method. *Monographs of the Society for Research in Child Development,* 1970, *35* (5, Serial No. 138).

Ypma, E. G. Prediction of the industrial creativity of research scientists from biographical information. Doctoral dissertation, Purdue University, 1968. *Dissertation Abstracts International,* 1970, *30,* 5731B–5732B. (University Microfilms No. 70-10,670.)

Zuckerman, H. A. Nobel laureates in the United States: A sociological study of scientific collaboration. Doctoral dissertation, Columbia University, 1965. *Dissertation Abstracts International,* 1968, *28,* 4294A–4295A. (University Microfilms No. 68-5664.)

Zuckerman, H. A. *Scientific elite: Nobel laureates in the United States.* New York: Free Press, 1977.

Name Index

Subject Index